THE HISTORY OF SWIN
AND SWINTON H

CH00687104

INTRODUCTIC

I have always marvelled at the architecture of the fine Regency building, Swinton Hall which dominates Fitzwilliam Street. Upon enquiry, I was astounded that so little was known about this building and its origins.

My good friend, Ken Wyatt and I always looked out for any information on it as we searched through various archival sources on other personal projects but over the years, came up with very little.

As often happened on landed estates, the productive economic times of the 18th and 19th centuries meant that many old historic halls were abandoned and these old fashioned, often draughty low ceiling buildings were replaced with state of the art, modern, larger successors. As Swinton had its own Hall dating back into very early times with a fine pedigree, it seemed a logical place to start. Had this happened here in Swinton? I soon established that, unfortunately, this was not the case and so the trail was still cold.

To this end, I decided the information must be out there somewhere and so, after hours of *ad hoc* searching, I eventually undertook a dedicated endeavour, determined to trace the history of the Hall right back. As I started to have some success, it clearly became evident why previous attempts had not been over fruitful; its history was so complex.

Life is never straight forward as people and their plans change generation by generation. This was clearly the situation in Swinton Hall's past. My research even took me out of the county to make enquiries and even to the other side of the world in order to answer certain abnormalities. Time, patience and luck all played their part but gradually, the story started to unfurl. My research had to delve even further back than the mere construction of Swinton Hall to fully explain the reasons for its origins and that turned up quite a bit of a surprise. Other people became as enthralled as I was and greatly assisted in searching out new information and going that extra mile to expand on its meaning. To this end, I am eternally grateful to Alan Downing, Ken Wyatt and Ron James, our Swinton Heritage archivist.

As is typical with wealthy families, the information became very legalistical and I needed my Chartered Management Accountant's head on to unscramble a lot of it. It is always said "the history of a house is not so much its bricks and mortar but the story of the people who lived in it". This is very much the case. I must warn you that as the people involved have been many, the story is very complex.

I am now pleased to be able to invite you to read the history of Swinton Hall, Swinton House and that very much of Swinton itself. Yours is now the easy part – please read on.

G H BREARLEY FCMA

ACKNOWLEDGEMENTS

I would like to thank the following for their assistance in the research and preparation of this book:-

Ron James – Swinton Heritage archivist
Richard Bailey – Ben Bailey Plc
Michael Brearley
The Staff at Retford Library especially Anna Hughes and C Kent
The kind lady in the post office at Clayworth
Ken Wyatt
Rotherham Local Studies Unit
Morgan Smith
Doug and Joyce Cavill
Alan Downing
Joanne Rayner (who has become a master at interpreting the most awful writing)
The Laird of Camster (for his undying support for our projects and archive material provided free)
Trevor James (Military Historian)
Swinton Library
James Rossi – Author and Retford District Local Historian
Margaret Harman and Alan Mills – State Library of Tasmania
Joseph C Bower (Roy)
Wath Parish Church
Wath Library
David and Joan Morley
Chris Barker
The Staff at Richmond Local Studies Unit (Surrey)
John Collins
Tickhill Church of St Mary's

Pedigree of Otter

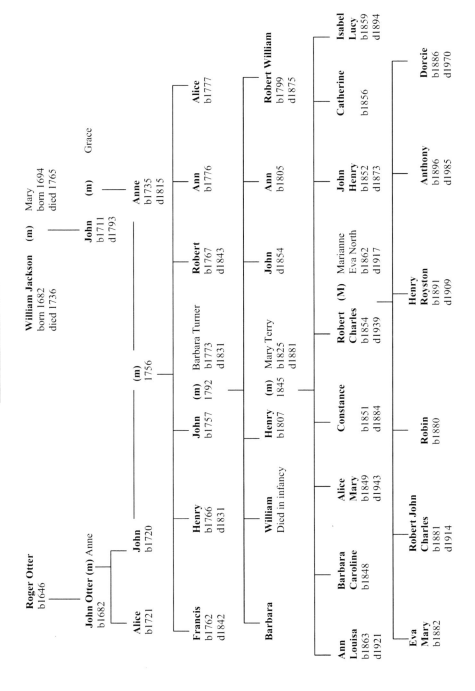

THE BEGINNING

In the first half of the 1700's, some sixty acres of Swinton's farming land were owned by a wealthy farming family from Wath called the Jacksons. They had a long pedigree of farming in the Wath area and were noted landowners. They had other major land interests around the Abdy area. They were noted as being the second largest land owners in Wath. John Jackson was the current head of the family and his wife was called Grace. John was born in 1711, the son of William and Mary Jackson. Their pedigree went back in Wath history for many generations. John Jackson and Grace had a daughter, Ann, who was born in 1735.

On 25 July 1756, daughter Anne Jackson, 21 years of age, married John Otter, 36 years of age, a gentleman. The sixty acre Estate at Swinton was passed over into the marriage as a dowry. John Otter had previously resided at the Royston Manor, Clayworth near Retford, Nottinghamshire. This was a fine Jacobean manor house of great character that had replaced an earlier Elizabethan manor and had been in the Otter family virtually since its construction. His father was also called John. They were a very wealthy family and large landowners receiving income from tenants and they also carried out their own farming activities.

The population of Clayworth at this time was around five hundred and seventy seven. The village was soon to be intercepted by the

Royston Manor, Clayworth, the Otter HQ.

Chesterfield canal and was bounded on the west by the River Idle. The Otters were the ruling land owners. The village Church at Clayworth is of eleventh century origin and contains many monuments to the Otter family inside.

Wath gentleman farmer, John Jackson had not only wanted his daughter to marry into the wealthy Otter family but he also wanted her to be accepted by them as a lady of means. The ownership of land then was indeed rare; there were only around twelve freeholders listed for the whole of Swinton at this time. With the exception of the Marquis of Rockingham and John Jackson, the others only owned small tracts of land. She was a bride with a treasure.

The population of Swinton in 1756 was around 375. There was probably a lot of talk around the village about this young couple who, against the grain, were starting out with so much wealth and now living in their midst. Anne was known as a co-heir, which meant she had a sister but no brothers and they would eventually share their father's estate.

The first task the newly wed couple set about at their new Swinton Estate was the construction of a home. This was not Swinton Hall but was Swinton House (the private club today) and was situated where their lands were dissected by Fitzwilliam Street, which was then the main road through the village of Swinton and was called High Street. The house was built in grand style and reflected the wealth available of the newly married couple. It was constructed as a large imposing

Here is seen Swinton Old Hall prior to its demolition. Unfortunately, no link was established between the earlier owners and the builders of Swinton Hall, which may have made research easier.

residence with servant's accommodation and set in large, walled grounds. It was built of dressed sandstone with a Welsh slate roof. Moulded cornice was used to form gutters. It had a five bay front with a triple wing to the rear. An attractive main entrance was at the front with a carriage drive leading right up to it. The doorway had a beautiful carved surround. Inside the large staircase was a centre piece of the house being lit by an impressive roof window. A coach house was also built in the grounds and there were extensive outbuildings, now all long gone.

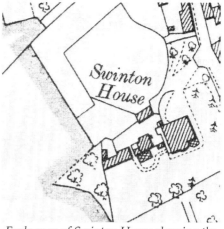

Early map of Swinton House showing the layout being very much different to that of today.

The Otters' Dowry land at Swinton extended over what are now part of the Comprehensive school playing fields, situated behind Swinton House and then extended into what is today Horsefair park and then out to where Temperance Street and Cliffield Road are to be found today. In 1756, these areas were part of Middle Shuttfield and Brookfield. The Otters also owned individual fields dotted around the village as part of the Estate like those at Upper Sparrowcliffe and towards Abdy.

The original front entrance to Swinton House can be seen here with its featured carved stone.

On 30 July 1757, the couple's first child was born who was named after his father, John. A second son, Francis, was born in 1762. A third son, Henry, was born in 1766 and a fourth son, Robert, was born in 1767. Daughters Anne and Alice were born in 1776 and 1777 respectively. What is certain is that although they all worked to extend the

3

The Duchess of Portland and her husband were great friends of the Otter family.

Swinton Estate, it was however, always seen as an annex of Clayworth, the true Otter seat of power. As evidence of this, most family celebrations, christenings and funerals nearly always took place at Clayworth and none at the Swinton village Chapel and only a few at the Church at Wath that served both villages. This is what had thwarted others when trying to research the history of the house. Swinton's early Church records show nothing at all.

Evidence of the high social standing of the Otter family can be found in the letters of Dorothy, Duchess of Portland, written from Welbeck Abbey and her London residence on Charles Street between 1767 and 1773 to her husband, the Duke of Portland. She often refers to people by their surname only but it is always "Mr Otter" when she is addressing John Otter at Clayworth. They had regular dining meetings and she turned to him for advice on various matters.

Another letter from the 2nd Earl of Moira to the 3rd Duke of Portland confirms he will agree to the Duke's request to have Otter made a Captain Lieutenant in the 28th Regiment. (The Otter referred to is John Otter's cousin.)

In another letter, the Duke uses his influence to help fifteen year old Charles Otter of Clayworth to move ships within His Majesty's Navy. His father had informed the Duke that "his ship is badly put together and his fellow mid-shipmen are a set of wild young fellows, some of who were under confinement for disobedience of orders". (Note the rank of mid-shipman at such a young age.)

It is believed that around 1780, following the earlier death of his father and upon the death of his mother,

The Duke of Portland

Swinton's John Otter inherited the Royston Manor Estate and moved back there with his wife, Anne.

In February 1789, John (Senior) died, leaving Anne, a widow who then apparently spent her time at Wath, Swinton and Clayworth.

Their eldest son, John, started courting a girl from Kilnhurst called Barbara Turner. Her father was William Turner. He was a landowner and resident at Kilnhurst Hall. They were duly married on 29 October 1792 at Rawmarsh and they moved into Swinton House.

Son John and his wife, Barbara, took over the running of the Swinton Estate. Anne then inherited further land, property and cash from her late father's Wath Estate following John Jackson's death in November 1793, which benefited the family greatly. The inheritance included the Wathwood Farm and lands.

As regards John and Barbara's marriage, they had six children. One child, a son (William), is believed to have died in infancy. The other children were daughters Barbara and Ann and sons John (Jnr) and Robert William who was born in 1799 and Henry who was born in 1807.

As time went by, the children all took different routes in life. John married into a wealthy family and Robert William went off to be a priest. He became land owner and incumbent at East Thorpe, six miles North West of Lincoln. The Gazette quotes, "The whole village lands are owned by John Robert Ealand apart from forty acres, which are owned by the Reverend Robert William Otter, BA, himself who resides at the Manor House". Ann went on to marry John Blackburn and they resided at Abdy. Barbara also married, and Henry we revisit.

A view of Swinton House Club today taken before the impending development, which is to take place in the grounds.

Swinton House - Part of the old Coach House, although still remaining today, will be dismantled to make way for the new development.

Of John's brothers and sisters, Alice and Ann went on to share a house at 67 Burlington Street, Wath upon Dearne. They lived comfortably along with a butler, a groom, a cook, a lady's maid, a housemaid and a kitchen maid. John's brother, Francis, became an attorney at Law and eventually became a barrister at Lincoln's Inn. His other brothers, Robert and Henry, lived at Wath.

SWINTON HALL

It was most likely John (Jnr) and Barbara who decided that the Swinton Estate (now increased with the Wath holdings of the Jackson's) could benefit from a new house, one that would be fitting of a rich Estate and be revered by the other nearby landowning families.

One thing that was very evident was that whilst the Otters were very wealthy, no titles were bestowed on them, which probably grated them. The Swinton Estate was important in that it abutted the lands of the renowned Wentworth Estate where Charles Watson-Wentworth, the 2nd Marquis of Rockingham and future Prime Minister, was assembling one of the largest, wealthiest Estates in the country. He was extremely powerful and it may have been good for the Otters to be nearby and in their neighbour's sight. The Marquis still had a lot of land in Swinton and was the village's benefactor. As Charles Watson-Wentworth increased his estates very successfully, he may have had more than a passing interest in the Otters especially as they abutted his inner jewel and HQ, his Wentworth Estate.

Charles Watson-Wentworth, 2nd Marquis of Rockingham (1730 - 1782), lagest landowner in the area and whose estates abutted the Otter lands.

The Otters had plans drawn up and circa 1800, it was decided to build a Hall in a semi-palladian Regency style. The house would be built at the opposite side of the road to Swinton House. The surrounding land at the side and rear would be used to make excellent parkland. A house of any substance would not be complete without its own parkland! The construction consisted of the Hall, a separate lodge with extensive attached stables, two staff cottages and an outdoor workshop and storage buildings.

The English Regency period commenced about 1790 and lasted until the 1830's. Regency buildings tended to have plenty of windows, giving light rooms. There was less detail on friezes and ceilings. "Neo Classical" was in vogue and things were designed with a classicism of form and shape. The Doric columns built in front of the main entrance are an example of this. The carved top stones give a flow of smoothness to the shape of the building. It was constructed of coursed dressed sandstone again with

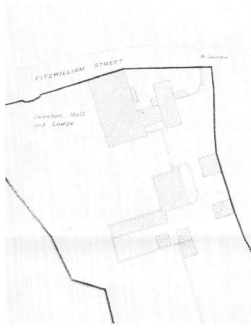

Early plans showing the layout of the Hall and buildings in its grounds.

cornice to form guttering. The upper cornice was moulded so that rain water would drop clear of the sandstone elevation. Gable stone copings were applied along with pilastered strips, flanking five tall windows to

The original carriage entrance into Swinton Hall.

8

the first floor. Furnishings of this time were based on plain walls adorned with paintings whilst the windows would have an abundance of drapery, elaborately looped and adorned with fringes.

The formal entrance to the Hall was through the gateway (still present) and a road swept round to the pillared front main entrance.

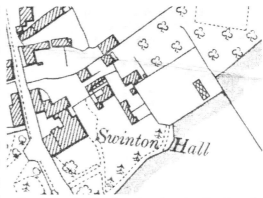

Further early drawing showing the situation of the Hall and the attached buildings.

Once you had alighted from the carriage, a footman would greet you at the entrance of the Hall. The carriage would then take a circular route either back out of the Hall onto Fitzwilliam Street or be handed to the horse keeper for looking after in the purpose built stables and the driver given accommodation above.

The Regency built Hall was much bigger than the Hall you see today. The Hall itself was around 9840 square feet. The downstairs and most of the second floor were day rooms. The second floor also had some bedroom suites. The upper third floor compromised of more family bedrooms and staff bedrooms as well as the children's bedrooms, next to where the nursery maid would sleep. The Hall, back then, had a large two storey T-shaped wing that housed the domestic quarters and the kitchens. The wing was large, being some 2931 square feet and in area, was 30% as big as the main Hall you see today. The structure was two storeys high and provided servants with living quarters in the upper parts. As was traditional, domestic servants' quarters were housed in a wing as opposed to being integral in the main house itself, with their own separate access so not to use the grandly designed entrance for the Hall itself, which was reserved for the owners.

The stable block and stores were also large. They covered about 4135 square feet. The horses were tethered in the stabling where about eight horses could be kept. The adjoining building is where the carriages were stored. This was about 40 feet by 50 feet. It is known that the block also contained upper storage and accommodation for the coachman and his family. Also built in the grounds were the small cottages and workshops for the estate. These were situated behind a stone wall that was built from the end of the coach house across to the Hall. A gateway was in the middle and once through it, there was a 760 square foot workshop and four staff cottages. The cottages were different in size with one being 634 square feet (family house), one of 475 square feet and two at 380 square feet.

The positioning of the wall meant that visitors to the house would enter a quadrangle and only see the main entrance to the Hall and the stables. Everything else, including the domestic wing, was screened off behind the wall. This also made it easy for servants and staff to freely pass up and down from their homes, out of sight of the family and visitors.

The Hall was generally screened from Fitzwilliam Street by the construction of a large sandstone wall, which was in excess of six feet high. The protrusion of the wing was subjected to further walling towards Fitzwilliam Street to make a kitchen garden that had a gated access onto the street. This entrance would have been used for deliveries and tradesmen visiting the Hall whilst on their duties. The large stone wall continued along Fitzwilliam Street to enclose what today is known as Horsefair Park. You can still see the lower quarter of the original wall. The grounds contained a large orchard and a pond. There are a large number of springs within this area.

The new construction was referred to as Swinton Hall so the existing Swinton Hall on Church Street became known as the Old Hall.

St Peter's Church, Clayworth, Notts – many memorials to the Otter family can be found in and around the church.

10

There was however, another unexpected twist in the story of Swinton Hall. Following his parents' death, son John (Jnr) and wife Barbara also returned to Clayworth. So now, they operated both from Clayworth and Swinton.

This event greatly affected the future of Swinton Hall. Although the Otters were the builders, John Otter and his wife Barbara, may never have moved into the house and it is suspected it was tenanted out on its completion or lived in by family members briefly then tenanted out shortly afterwards.

The tenanting out of estates was common practice then as land did not change ownership that often and there was always a demand from sons of wealthy people with the ability to pay a market rent. The Otters' children themselves tenanted various other estates around the family's freehold Clayworth property.

The tenants would furnish the Hall quite lavishly and move in complete with an entourage of servants and other staff of coachman and gardeners.

The Otters did continue to acquire further land for the Swinton Estate when in 1816, they took land through the Swinton enclosures. The enclosures were the appropriation of common land into private ownership. The first Enclosure Act was in 1603. Hardship was initially caused as strip farming was carried out on the Commons by the village families for growing food. The rationale behind the land seizures was so that agriculture could be modernised and the highway infrastructure upgraded. The Swinton Enclosure Act 1815 stated:-

"And whereas there are within the Township of Swinton, several open common fields and individual enclosures, containing together by estimation four hundred and twenty acres, and there area also within the said Township of Swinton several commons and parcels of waste ground containing together by estimation 420 acres or thereabouts and whereas the Right Honourable Wm Wentworth Fitzwilliam, Earl Fitzwilliam is Lord of the Manor or reputed Lord of the Manor of Swinton, aforesaid, and in right thereof is entitled to the soil of the said several commons and parcels of waste ground within the said Township. And whereas the said Earl Fitzwilliam and others are respectively owners and proprietors of lands and grounds lying within the said several open common fields and undivided enclosures within the said Township of Swinton "they exclusively" are entitled to right of common or waste ground within the Township." The others referred to include the Otters.

Commissioners were appointed to be in charge of the Land Enclosure. They had the right to stop up any roads, which went through an enclosure.

Any land marked with baulks which had previously been ploughed was to be classed as field land for due enclosure.

The land had to be enclosed within six months of the passing of the act by fences. Gates and Styles, which were to be the responsibility of the new owners of the fields.

It was noted that Ann Otter (formerly Jackson) was awarded part of the middle shut field, which was behind Swinton House. The land she was awarded stretched right up to Swinton Common Road (now called Wentworth Road), widening out as it neared the far boundary. She was also awarded 50% of the dyke furlong, which abutted up to where Queen Street is today. She was also awarded extensive land in Upper Sparrowcliffe field, which today is known as Highthorn. Ann wouldn't have seen much benefit for the newly established estate extension as she died on 14 October 1815, aged 80. Her memorial in Wath Church was inscribed "Her desire to distress was unbounded".

A fine memorial to the Otters inside St Peter's Church, Clayworth.

As the enclosure documentation also refers to the Misses Otter (being Ann and Alice) who are living at Wath upon Dearne, we assume that they are perhaps living in one of the former old Jackson properties and thus, Swinton House was now vacated, perhaps also tenanted.

Ann and Alice Otter along with their brother, John Otter still residing at Clayworth, commenced legal action on 6 March 1822 to evict an occupier of some of the land they had been awarded. It is noted they were successful and gained back the occupancy. I suppose there would be some deep resentment by some people at losing what they thought was theirs by right. After the death of John, the Hall was entrusted into the safe keeping of his surviving, still unmarried daughters, Barbara, Alice and Ann and Francis, his second son, whom he had chosen to be his heir. Francis had also had some land allocated to him under the Enclosures Act.

By this time, the youngest son, Henry, was living in Lincoln. Ann had now moved to Caenby in Lincolnshire but was still unmarried and son Robert had been in Lincoln but had recently moved back to Wath.

St Peter's Church, Clayworth – this is known as the Otter window.

The tenant of Swinton Hall in 1822 was the Reverend Henry Bowen Cooke. He was newly married. He originated from Darfield and was born on 29 March 1797. His wife, Juliana Mary Serjeantson, was also from Darfield. They were married on 27 June 1822 at All Saint's Church, Darfield, and they probably moved straight into the Hall. Their first child was born on 8 September 1825 and was christened Edward. It is believed that Henry Cooke may have become an incumbent, as often happened to the youngest son of gentry. He was obviously from a family of means in order to take on the commitment of running Swinton Hall. He had left the Hall by 1833.

John and Anne's daughter, Ann Otter died in 1830 and Alice, Barbara and Frances continued holding the Swinton Estate as joint trustees.

The new tenant of the Hall in 1833 was Charles Faber. He was born in Calverley, Leeds in 1777. He had married Martha and they had a son, Charles Wilson, born in 1814 and daughters, Ann Sophia and Elizabeth

Sarah. Two other children died in infancy. They were a family who enjoyed some success although it is not known how they established their fortune. Charles Faber had lived in the village previously, having been made an elected Church Warden in 1816 and was the first warden to serve the newly built Church of St Margaret's. He was the uncle of Frederick William Faber, the famous hymn writer and author. His most famous hymn was "Hark, Hark My Soul". He was one of the early followers of the Oxford movement but later became a Catholic. As a boy, he stayed at Swinton with his uncle and worshipped there. Tragedy struck the Fabers when, in 1834, only one year after moving into Swinton Hall, wife Martha died. Of their children, Charles Wilson went on to marry into the Fontayne family who lived at High Melton Hall. Elizabeth Sarah married a Robert Stanton Scholfield and they resided at Sand Hall. Robert Schofield was a former Eton schoolboy and was practicing as a barrister of Lincoln's Inn. Ann Sophia married the Reverend William Henry Elliott, who was vicar of Stainton in Cleveland.

It was around this time another Otter descendent moved into the village. He was Robert Otter-Blythman. His father, Joseph Blythman

St Peter's Church, Clayworth - Otter's corner, which is full of family memorials.

from Bawtry, had married Mary Otter of Royston Manor, Clayworth back in 1787. Robert was born somewhat later in the marriage on 5 February 1803 and his surname reflected both sides of the family. Robert took up medical studies and qualified as a doctor of medicine. He went on to become a surgeon. He was married to Catherine Simmons at Wentworth Church in 1830. He resided on what is now known as Milton Street but was then called "Well Street" because of the proximity of the village well. Robert provided medical services to the Swinton area. This was run entirely as a private practice

Early members of the Otter family are interred close to the St Peter's Church, Clayworth in elaborate graves.

as obviously, there was not a National Health Service. Villagers entered into savings clubs, paying a small amount each so as to have a fund to pay the doctor for medical services.

Robert Otter-Blythman and Catherine had four children, Catherine, born 28 September 1835, Charles Henry, born 28 September 1836, Arthur, born 18 February 1841 and lastly, Clement Samuel, born 20 February 1844. Clement Blythman followed in his father's footsteps and also qualified as a doctor and a surgeon. He became the Medical Officer of Health to the Swinton Board, serving from 1876 to 1883. He continued administering to people's medical needs into the 1900's. He also became Chairman of the Rate Payers Committee and was well respected in the community.

The elderly son of the original John and Anne, Robert Otter – gentleman – appears in White's directory of 1835 with the indication he has land interests in Wath and Swinton. Robert died in August 1843, aged 76.

The 1841 census confirms that Swinton House was now tenanted by 40 year old James Nelson, a railway contractor along with his wife Marianne and two children, Thomas aged 4 and John aged 2 along with servant, Hannah Shaw.

The railways were in their infancy and much activity was underway to lay down the lines for the competing railways. The first railway line was opened through the town of Swinton on 30 June 1840 with the new Swinton Station being constructed and opened at the same time. James Nelson would most likely have been heavily involved. He was living in grand style and was obviously influential. He would most likely move on as the work advanced. This is held out in that in 1844, it was noted in White's directory that John Staniforth-Beckitt, iron founder, was now residing at Swinton House. He was formerly of Conisbrough and was described as being "a gent". He was involved in various land deals and mortgages often with a Francis Marchant, MD, of Hemsworth, to whom we believe he was related.

It was around this time that Charles David Faber left Swinton Hall and moved in with his daughter but a new tenant was soon found by the Otters.

This vacancy was filled when, in 1844, the elderly Miss Eleanor Beckitt, became the resident of Swinton Hall along with two live-in domestic servants. She was listed as being a "land and property owner" and being self sufficient with income from annuities and dividends. It was noted in the Church minute records, that Eleanor Beckitt was a strong minded lady parishioner who was occasionally known to put up her parasol in church if a particularly sunny morning, as the sunlight shone strongly through the windows. The blinds previously fitted had deteriorated and no-one was yet putting their hand in their pocket to fund new ones so the Church would echo to the sound of Miss Beckitt's parasol being snapped up and down. It is minuted the ritual was repeated years later when the new blinds were taken down for cleaning. Eleanor Beckitt was born in 1787, originating from Barnsley. She obviusly had little patience and would stand for no inconvenience. The story of Swinton Hall now has to side step.

Known Tenants of Swinton Hall

1822 – 1833	-	Reverend Henry Bowen-Cooke
1833 – 1844	-	Charles Faber
1844 – 1864	-	Miss Eleanor Beckitt
1864 – 1877	-	Major Edward B Cooke (Jonathan White)
1880 – 1885	-	Edward Barker
1885 – 1887	-	Rachel Barber
1887 – 1892	-	James White
1892 – 1894	-	Robert Marsh
1894 – 1902	-	John Grayson Lowood
1903 – 1935	-	Joseph Aquilla Bower

The Tenants of Swinton House

1841 – 1844	-	James Nelson
1844 – 1852	-	John Staniforth-Beckitt
(1852 – 1888)	-	The Otter Family (the owners) resided
1888 – 1900 ©	-	Augustus James Fenner
1901 -		Henry Pearson

HENRY OTTER

Henry, the son of John and Barbara Otter, was thought of with great affection by his aunts at Wath upon Dearne and his uncle, Francis who was, by this time, living at Ranby Hall. Henry's future was still to be mapped out and they were to help. They collectively took legal advice and established a trust for the Swinton Estate with nephew Henry being made the future beneficiary. Henry, as the youngest of his line, may obviously have not fared so well in the inheritance stakes and it was a way of looking after him. Not dis-similar today, the gentry always enter into detailed planning for estate succession. The Clayworth Estate and other lands presumably took care of Henry's other brothers.

In the trust document, it is mentioned that upon the marriage of Henry, the Estate at Swinton comprising of two mansion houses, other tenements and sixty acres plus of land, was to be granted for 100 years for free use by Henry and his new wife. In addition, the trust was to also award an annual allowance to his new wife to assist in the running costs of the Hall. The Trust also allowed his new wife and any children they had to become beneficiaries upon Henry's death. It is clear from

All Saints Parish Church of Wath upon Dearne is home to some of the Swinton and Wath Otter family memorials.

Memorial to Anne Otter and Robert Otter, situated inside Wath Church.

the creation of this Trust, there was a real desire by the Otters to restore Swinton Hall back to some security with an Otter in residence to hopefully carry on into the future.

In 1845, 38 year old Henry Otter married Miss Mary Terry, daughter of William Terry of Bath, Somerset and Rugby, Northamptonshire; she was seventeen years his junior. For his education, Henry had been sent to the Rugby School and it is believed that whilst there, he may have met the family. Mary Terry herself came from a prestigious background with her family owning a large amount of property.

As a young man, Henry loved sports and actively took part in them, receiving several severe injuries along the way. He liked riding as did his wife and they used to support the fox hunts at Clayworth.

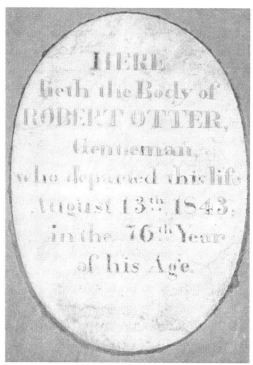

Robert Otter appears to have been interred inside the parish church at Wath.

After Henry Otter got married however, he moved first to Tickhill. This was because both the Swinton properties were still tenanted by the Beckett's. Although back then, the Beckitts did not have the protection of the Landlord and Tenant Act, the Otters decided to let them stay. As Henry and his new wife were the only beneficiaries, one assumes that the rents payable would have been given to Henry possibly to pay rent on the property at Tickhill. Alternatively, it may have been part of the Otter empire.

Henry and his new wife moved to 149 Northgate, Tickhill, which was an imposing residence next door to the home of the Reverend Edward Hawks-Brooksbank, MA, both being situated at the side of the Church. They lived at the house along with a nurse, a cook, a housemaid, a nursery maid and a groom. Other members of the Otter family were also resident in Tickhill.

Unfortunately, the residence is no longer standing and all that remains is the large stone wall that once surrounded it. It is believed that the Reverend was related to Henry. The 1851 census lists Henry as being a "Landed Proprietor" and Edward simply as being the "Vicar of Tickhill".

It is noted that Edward appears as a Trustee in various Otter family Trusts and so, if he was not related, he was very well known and trusted. He has been the town's vicar since 1822, having been born in Tickhill. He lived in the vicarage along with his wife and children and various servants and was actually a wealthy man himself. The deliverance of religion to the masses was, in these times, the preserve of the gentry.

In 1848, Henry and Mary's first child, Barbara Caroline was born. Also, on 17 March 1848, Edward Brookbank and Robert John Pettiward were appointed trustees to the Swinton Trust. Mr Pettiward was Henry's wife, Mary's cousin. He was born in 1819, the son of the Lord of the Manor of great Finborough, which is situate three miles North West of Stowmarket in the County of Suffolk. He took over as Lord of the Manor on his father's death. Robert John Pettiward was a very wealthy man indeed. His residence was Finborough Hall and the grounds included a huge lake, some 140 acres in extent. He had nine servants living in the Hall itself, these being a butler, housekeeper, footman, cook, kitchen assistants and parlour maids. His coach staff, gamekeepers, etc, lived in cottages in the grounds. He owned extensive farming land roundabout and also owned a lot of property in London in the Putney and Kensington areas.

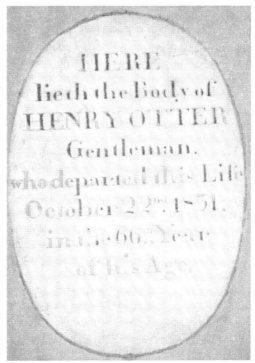

As also does his brother, Henry Otter.

On one street alone, he owned fifty one houses all in a row. Today, these properties command prices of over a million pounds each.

He was eleven years younger than Henry Otter but they were presumably very close. Pettiward's wife was called Francis and they had four daughters. It is known their respective daughters socialised. He was perhaps included as a trustee to the Otters' Swinton Trust to possibly represent his cousin Mary's interest in the Trust's operations. Mary's nephew, Charles Terry, eventually changed his surname to Pettiward in order to inherit the Pettiward Estate on Robert's death in 1908.

Whilst still at Tickhill, 1849 saw the arrival of Henry and Mary's second child, Alice Mary and in 1851, their third child, Constance was born.

In 1852, John Beckett left Swinton House, which then enabled Henry, aged 45, and wife Mary to move, at last, onto the Swinton Estate. They may have initially chosen to occupy Swinton House as a temporary measure due to the continuing tenanting of Swinton Hall, with the idea of then moving into the Hall upon it becoming vacant.

In 1852, John Henry was born being not only Henry and Mary's first

Otter memorials in situ at Wath parish church.

son but also, the first child to be born at Swinton. Henry's aunts, Alice and Ann, living at Wath, made part of their income from money lending. Alice, through her legal advisors, Felix and Francis Nicholson of Nicholson Solicitors, Wath, set up a trust fund and they acted as her trustees. In 1850, Alice loaned £2500 to Hoole France, Mary Haigh, Jane Badger, James Wilson, George Nicholson and Richard Beckitt. She took charge on a freehold estate at Harworth as security. She advanced them another £500 in 1853. They had to pay her interest on the loans monthly in advance. This loan was fully paid back on 4 June 1853 but another loan was about to go all wrong. It was a large loan and Henry and the Nicholson Solicitors all became involved in the summer of 1853.

Some five years earlier, Alice had loaned £4700 to a group of people, Joseph Thackray of Leeds, a wool merchant, Anne Louise Gossip, Georgina Gossip and Susanna Gossip, all of Hatfield (near Doncaster), for a business venture. All did not go well and in April 1853, Alice commenced recovery proceedings of the security being held. This must have been quite a venture as for the times, it was a huge sum of money.

Alice now relied on her nephew to help organise the complex case for her, which Henry did. The case had complications and counterclaims

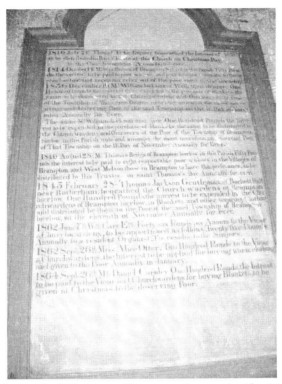

Inside the parish church of Wath upon Dearne can be seen the Charities Board, which records donations and bequests left by parishioners for the needy. Entry of 26 September 1862 refers to Miss Alice Otter.

but was successful, and the following Hatfield properties previously pledged as security were added to the Otter empire:-

BOW WINDOW HOUSE	TENEMENT
Adam Field Close	4.1 acres
Old Farm Close	2.2 acres
Windmill and Lands on Mill Close	4.1 acres
Dwelling House at the Lings	20.5 acres
Field on the Lings	2.5 acres
Netherholme Close	5.0 acres
House in Hatfield Woodhouse and	
Adjoining Field	11.1 acres
Piper Lane Close, Hatfield	2.5 acres
Lings Common, Hatfield	6.5 acres

The sheer size of this cash loan demonstrates the wealth that the Otters of Swinton and Wath enjoyed.

In 1854, Henry and Mary's second son, Robert Charles was born at Swinton House. 1856 saw the arrival of daughter Catherine and 1859 saw the arrival of daughter Isabella Lucy and in 1863, their last child, Ann, was born. The Otters were very active in life around Swinton but still kept their close connection with the Clayworth Estate, the Otter "HQ".

At the tender age of five, eldest son John Henry, was sent away to commence his formal education. He was sent as a boarder to King Edward VI Grammar School in Bury St Edmunds, Suffolk. The school was originally found in 1550 by Edward VI along with several other men of eminence. Previous pupils had included Archbishop Sancroft, dramatist Richard Cumberland, Sir Samuel Romilly, Dr Blomfield (Bishop of London) and the Earls of Albermarle. The school was considered to be a feeder school for Oxford and Cambridge Universities. The school looked after boys from the age of five right up to university entrance. Leaving home at such an early age must have been traumatic for the child and the practice would, today, be frowned upon by most. Despite the name, "Free Grammar School", it was anything but free and demonstrates Henry considered his family worthy of the best and were not to be "also rans".

Henry started expanding the Estate by building more houses and cottages to increase the rent roll. It was in the 1860's that Henry erected numbers 26 to 37 Fitzwilliam Street, being twelve dwelling houses. The row of properties later became known as "Bobby's Row" after one of the early tenants was one of the town's policemen.

Henry had also built a group of fifteen cottages, situated across from Mirfield Cottage, which was also on Fitzwilliam Street. Later, he also cut a road from Station Road, calling it Temperance Street. He had built there forty two dwellings. None of these remain today as they were all demolished and now, old people's bungalows sit on the site. These dwellings were on the right hand side looking up and also on the opposite side, perpendicular to the street in a straight row actually encroaching into what was previously part of the Swinton Hall's parkland. If Henry had been living in Swinton Hall and not Swinton House, the later development would probably not have taken place.

In 1860, Henry took the legal oath and was appointed as a West Riding Magistrate, eventually becoming Chairman of the Rotherham Bench. He sat at the Court House on College Street that had been purpose built in 1825. Every Monday, Henry attended the petty sessions of the upper divisions of Strafforth and Tickhill to give law to the people. He also sat at the monthly County Court for amounts disputed up to £50. He also sat at the quarter sessions on more serious cases. The Quarter Sessions was the principle Court of the Magistrates. They held cases where a jury was present. (They are today replaced by the Crown Court.) His fellow magistrates sitting at these sessions included John Fullerton of Thrybergh Hall. Another duty of the magistrates then was to also supervise the provision of local prison facilities, overlook the local police force and to act as a public registry, ratifying railway awards, etc.

Henry had extensions built onto the Swinton House property to make it more lavish. Whilst doing these, he also had a holding cell constructed within Swinton House where a prisoner could be held. The traces of this can still be seen today at the rear.

It was intended that local prisoners would be held there, awaiting transportation to the York assizes when it was felt their offence merited a more serious punishment administered by the York High Court. All the duties of the magistrate would have kept Henry very busy. He was also connected to the District Board of Guardians at Rotherham who had their inaugural meeting on 3 July 1837 with the Earl Fitzwilliam elected in the chair. The Board bought five acres of land from the Rotherham Feoffees and built a huge new workhouse abutting Alma Road. Henry sat with thirty other guardians to help trustee the operation. There was, at its peak, around two hundred inmates. A report in 1867 stated Rotherham workhouse housed one hundred and forty old and infirm and sixty children. Only one nurse oversaw them all. Conditions in the workhouses were designed to act as a deterrent for all but the genuinely destitute.

The previous decade had seen a new kind of coal mining emerge; the large deep mined super pits. The old methods of mining were being thrown out of the window as new technology in ventilation and machinery meant the deep, previously untouchable coal seams could be reached for rich pickings. The new coal companies needed to negotiate with land owners, a deal everyone was happy with.

A deal meant the mining company could get at the coal and the land owners had their pockets lined. All round Swinton, new collieries were being sunk. Various collieries were interested in Swinton's coal. The landowners found themselves being "courted" by the independent mining companies to swing the deal. For the rich, it was money for old rope.

In 1860, Henry started negotiations with the mining company, J and T

Charlesworth's to lease them the mineral rights for the lands under the Swinton Estate. Charlesworth's wanted to extend their reserves for the new Thyrbergh Hall Colliery (later called Kilnhurst Colliery) whose shafts were sunk in 1858 down to the Barnsley seam. Henry entered into a thirty five year lease. They paid him an annual rent and a royalty per ton mined; more income for the gentleman.

It was a mini boom time for the expanding village of Swinton and everyone was jumping on the band wagon. Even Dr Clement S Blythman sold the Barnsley bed coal under his house and surgery for £96 9s 4d. The Reverend Arthur Blythman living at Hennington, sold a large tract of coal under land he owned near Post Office Lane, Swinton, fetching £287 17s 6d. Even the coal under the Glebe land was sold by the Church.

The 1861 census show the Otter family had imported a governess, Elizabeth Hardy, and had domestic staff, which consisted of Mary Johnson (servant), Harriet Gillian (housemaid), Isabel Hall (nursery maid), Elisa Metcalf (assistant nursery maid), Henry Battersby (groom) and Samual Ward (driver).

As Henry got older, his old sports injuries pained him and he was kept from any active pursuits. His lifelong active participation in fox hunting had to cease. He was attended to medically by Dr Blythman. Henry lived at Swinton House as a gentleman, served the community and was well respected in the area. Henry and his wife were very benevolent to charitable needs around the area.

It was in 1861 that son John Henry's education at Bury St Edmund's came to an end and he moved on to the Marlborough School, still as a boarder. It is not known why he was moved but the school was classed as even more prestigious than Bury St Edmund's. It had a long history and a fine pedigree of former pupils.

Front of Marlborough College where the Otter sons attended.

It is known that Henry and Mary had a wide circle of friends. In Swinton, they were close to the Blythman's and also counted Mr and Mrs Alfred Bagguley as friends. Alfred was formerly a Rockingham Pottery artist/ decorator and along with his father, formed a new pottery operation with the finished works marked "Bagguley". The wares were decorated with what was known as the "Bagguley Brown Glaze", a secret formula developed by Alfred's father who was originally a Staffordshire potter who moved to South Yorkshire for better prospects with the Bramelds and the Rockingham Pottery.

Within the gentry, they were close to George Cooke-Yarborough of Campsmount, Campsall. He was the son of John Cooke, gentleman of Streetshorpe (now Edenthorpe) who took the surname of Cooke-Yarborough on inheriting the Yarborough Estates from his spinster aunts. George, like Henry, served as a county magistrate and was accredited with owning 2894 acres of land. They were also close to the Ward – Aldams' of Frickley Hall. They held estates totalling 3103 acres, mainly in Yorkshire but with some further land in Scotland and Lincolnshire. They were classed as "new money on the block" having earned their fortunes in earlier generations of industrialists. Henry was also good friends with Admiral Douglas who was a former King's Naval Commander and then the Earl Fitzwilliam's land agent.

Sadly, on 29 February 1864, Miss Eleanor Beckett, after 20 years tenancy at Swinton Hall, died. This now gave Henry the choice of whether to move into the Hall himself but he chose not to. Had he been younger, he may well have done but he was probably too settled at Swinton House and didn't want the upheaval. Instead, he created a new tenancy in favour of Major Edward B Cook and also for a Johnathan White to occupy separate accommodation in the grounds.

On Easter day in 1865, following the death of the last of the trustees, Miss Alice Otter, the remaining trustees decided that the Swinton Estate should revert to Henry Otter in his own right so he now became the freeholder of the Swinton Estate.

Just prior to her death, Alice set up her own charity for the needy of Wath and Swinton Parish. She paid £200 into the charity and it was administered by the vicar of Wath and the Church wardens. Nicholson, Saunders and Nicholson Solicitors controlled the investment and the interest was used to purchase warm clothing and blankets for the poor in the winter.

In 1865, Henry became embroiled in what was known as the "Wath General Election Riots". The previous election was held in 1859 and so Lord Palmerstone decided it was to be in July 1865 that the voters should again have their say. Times were moving on and people didn't want to hang onto the staunch early Victorian doctrines but they wanted to see changes.

Unfortunately, the majority were not allowed to use the ballot box as the voting system was still governed by the Great Reform Act of 1832, which meant in the Wath district for example, only 471 eligible voters were allowed. This district covered Adwick, Barnburgh, Billingley, Bolton, Darfield, Denaby, Houghton, Mexborough, Swinton, Thurnscoe and Wombwell. Only three percent of the people were eligible to vote. They were all landowners and people with a high income.

For the first time in election history, the West Riding was to be separated into North and South constituencies, each returning two MP's. Whilst this was an acknowledgement that the population of the West Riding was growing, there were seeds of unrest as the large numbers of labourers in the local industries also wanted their voices to be heard. Whilst their opinions and views were encouraged, they could not participate at the ballot box.

The Liberal candidates were Viscount Milton of Wentworth Woodhouse and Henry Beaumont from London. The Conservative candidates were Christopher Beckitt Denison of Doncaster and Walter Spencer Stanhope of Cannon Hall, Barnsley. Between 200 and 400 people thronged the Wath streets making voters pass through them. Voters wore rosettes and so were easily identified. Initially, the abuse was verbal but after 1.00pm, it descended into violence.

Henry Otter and his cousin, Robert of Gainsborough, arrived in Wath by carriage, which parked at the rear of the Red Lion public house, where they alighted and went into the Conservative Committee room set up in the pub itself.

They managed to get to the ballot box and placed their votes for the Conservatives and then left.

Later on, the crowd smashed most of the Red Lion's windows, stoned the police and assaulted arriving voters with mob violence. Only forty four men of the possible 471 actually voted. Many others probably turned back after seeing what confronted them. The police struggled to keep any order at all. As one of the voters split his vote, the result for Wath was announced as Conservatives, 24 and Liberals, 22. The Wath result however, was only a small cog as all the votes in the Southern division had to be totalled up. The final result was Milton (Liberal) – 7258, Beaumont (Liberal) – 6925, Denison (Conservative) – 6884 and Stanhope (Conservative) – 6819.

The events of the day were extremely disturbing to Henry but as the justice machine gathered pace, rioters were duly arrested by the police to come before the Courts. And who was sitting on the bench to judge them? None other than Henry Otter, JP, FJS Foljambe, MP and Reverend W Howard. This was on Saturday, 5 August. Twenty three men were brought before the bench. There should have been twenty four but one had fled to America in the meantime to start a new life.

Of the men, the bench discharged six with no real evidence, another seven were proven not guilty, three were bound over for one year with a £20 penalty, and seven were given short jail sentences after being adjourned to the quarter sessions.

1866 saw son John Henry move on from the Marlborough School up to Trinity College at Oxford University. He made up one of the 300 freshmen who started there in October. The College was founded by Thomas Pope. It still exists today and is on a spacious site, built round four quadrangles. The College's former pupils included the First Earl of Chatham (William Pitt) and later pupils included First Earl of Stanhope, Jeremy Thorpe, Norris McWhirter and Richard Burton.

In 1868, there was a big celebration at Swinton House when eldest daughter, Barbara, married the Reverend Alfred William Wickham Davies. He was born in Langford, Berkshire, in 1825. After formal education, he went into the Church, becoming Curate at Harkness in Yorkshire. He was another example of a younger son of gentry entering the Church.

For a change, Henry decided not to use Clayworth's Church but instead, the home Church of St Margaret's was to be utilised. This was a big event for Swinton and flags and garlands were suspended from many windows in celebration. A large crowd of people gathered and the schools were closed for the day so the children could witness the spectacle. Barbara worked with the local schools, donating some of her time to assist in educating the children. She was popular. The bride and her father were taken the short distance to the Church by carriage. People thronged the streets, cheering.

After the ceremony, a company of girls who had strewn flowers down the Church path, walked in front of the new couple, laying down even more flowers in their wake. The whole assemblage cheered them. This wedding demonstrates the popularity and status of the Ottter family in Swinton. The new couple moved, shortly afterwards, to Devon as Alfred was made assistant Curate at the Lustleigh Parish Church of St John the Baptist.

In 1870, an account of Henry Otter's cousin, Henry Charles Otter's naval career was published to celebrate his retirement. He joined His Majesty's Navy in 1822, rising up to a Commander by August 1844. He had commanded "The Sparrow", "The Avon" and "The Comet", patrolling the Scottish and Irish coasts. On 8 September 1854, he became Captain of "Alban" and took part in the Russian War in the Baltic, being praised for his bravery and cunning of command. He then captained "Fire Fly" in 1855 and took part in further naval hostile engagement. He continued on in the Royal Navy, rising up to Rear Admiral before finally retiring in 1870. He was then awarded the "Order of Bath" in recognition of his naval achievements.

The 1871 census records show the tenancies of Swinton Hall unchanged and as follows:-

SWINTON HALL			OCCUPATION	BIRTH PLACE
Mjr Edward B Cooke	Head	M 44	Adjutant Volunteer	Yorks
Marianne J Cooke	Wife	M 38	Wife	Kirby Fleetham, Yorks
Rosabella J Cooke	Dau	U 6	Swinton, Yorks	
Evelyn J Cooke	Dau	U 3	Swinton, Yorks	
Elizabeth Avery	Ser	U 35	Domestic Servant	Skegby, Notts
Sarah Brown	Ser	U 31	Domestic Servant	Brampton, Derbys
Marrion Weldon	Ser	U 22	Domestic Servant	Radbourne, Derbys
Lucy White	Ser	U 14	Domestic Servant	Darlton, Notts

COTTAGE ATTACHED TO SWINTON HALL STABLES

John Green		Head	U 34	Groom & Coachman	Newcastle on Tyne

PART OF SWINTON HALL GROUNDS

Jonathon White	Head	M 68	Retired Milkman	*Barmborough, Yorks
Ann White	Wife	M 58	Wife	*Barmborough, Yorks
Annie Newsam	Ser	U 18	Domestic Servant	Bolton on Dearne, Yorks

*NB Today, Barmborough is today known as Barnborough

Major Edward Bowen Cooke was the same Edward who was actually born at Swinton Hall in 1825. He had now returned to take tenancy himself. Although his mother had died in 1857, his father was still alive but in retirement from the clergy.

The Sheffield Regiment of the 4th West Yorkshire Rifle Volunteers was raised on 30 September 1859. Edward Cook joined them on 8 April 1863 as a Captain Adjutant. He had enjoyed a military career previously and oversaw the progress and training of the new volunteer force. He was promoted to the rank of major and remained with them until 1873 when, at the age of forty six, he retired. It is known he got on well with the Otter family and they mixed socially. Their respective children were also apparently firm friends.

The census for Swinton House of 1871 shows:-

NAME	YEAR BORN	POSITION	BIRTH PLACE
Henry Otter	1808	Head	Clayworth, Notts
Alice Mary Otter	1849	Daughter	Tickhill, Yorks
Constance Otter	1851	Daughter	Tickhill, Yorks
Catherine Otter	1856	Daughter	Swinton, Yorks
Isabel L Otter	1859	Daughter	Swinton, Yorks
Anne L Otter	1863	Daughter	Swinton, Yorks
Emelie A Carttan	1837	Governess	Greenwich, Kent
Samuel Owen	1827	Servant	Middle, Shropshire
Harriett Richards	1810	Servant	Albury, Surrey
Agnes Shaw	1849	Servant	Newcastle on Tyne
Sarah Womack	1835	Servant	Wath on Dearne, Yorks
Mary Osborne	1854	Servant	Dalton Brook, Yorks

Henry's wife, Mary, was obviously away on the census day.

Barbara was, by now, living at Hindley Hall, Wigan. Her husband was carrying out Chaplin duties for the wealthy Leigh Rogers & Co Ltd, coal proprietors. They later moved into Bradshaw Hall.

Henry's son, Robert Charles had now, like his elder brother, been sent into education and so was not present on Census Day. He also went to Marlborough and Trinity College. He played for the school XI football team and was a keen sportsman, as was his father before him. He was also a keen horseman. Whilst living at Swinton, he learned to ride and as a youngster, attended local fox hunts. At the time of the 1871 Census, Robert was lodging at 14 Royal Parade, Blackheath, Lewisham in Kent. He was registered as a student and would have been attending Trinity College near Greenwich.

The 1873 National Survey Land Return of all landowners in England and Wales, shows that Henry Otter had, in his own name, ownership of 130 acres of land. The executors of his deceased sister showed that the land in Miss Otters' Trust ownership with Henry as beneficiary, amounted to 133 acres. Interestingly, the Earl Fitzwilliam was recorded as owning 19164 acres (excluding the Irish Estate).

Robert Blythman's Estate also owned eleven acres of Swinton's Land. The Reverend Brooksbank, still in Tickhill, was credited with owning 197 acres of land himself.

Tragedy came to the Otter family in 1873 when the eldest son, John Henry, unexpectedly died. This was on the 6 May. He had left Oxford University previously and he was embarking on a world tour and was at Hobart Town, Tasmania when tragedy befell him. He died in his lodgings at Hampden Road, Battery Point. He had caught a chill, which developed into pneumonia. He was still a bachelor. He was buried in the Cornelian Bay Cemetery Church of England Section. This now meant that the heir to the Swinton Estate became second son, Robert Charles.

After leaving Trinity College, Robert went on to a partial military career, firstly with the 2nd Nottinghamshire and later with the 4th Nottinghamshire Sherwood Foresters Regiment. On 28 January 1880, he married Marianne Eva North, the eldest daughter of Charles North of Rougham Hall, Norfolk. She was eight years his junior. No doubt this would have been a major celebration in the Otter household. She was the great, great, great, great, great granddaughter of none other than King Charles II. Her forbear was a member of the aristocracy and also the King's mistress. She was originally from French aristocracy and was placed in the household of King Charles' II sister. Following a visit to see the King at Dover, he placed her as a lady in waiting to the Queen in his own Palace. I wonder what King Charles' sister made of that!

It has been common through the centuries for Kings to sire children outside a marriage. These children were not heirs to the throne; heirs were born of the official Queen. Louise Rebee de Penancoet had a son on 29 July 1672. He was given the name of Charles Lennox and

Louise Rebee de Penancoet, Mistress of Charles the 2nd and Marianne Eva North's forebear.

Charles the 2nd.

he was so bestowed the title of the Duke of Richmond and Lennox in 1675. This was the King's way of acknowledging his child.

Charles Lennox married Anne Brudnell in 1692 and they had a daughter, Anne who was born in 1703. She married William Anne Keppel, the 2nd Earl of Keppel. (He was given Anne as a middle name in honour of Queen Anne.) Their child was the famous Admiral Augustus Keppel. He was a close friend of Charles, Marquis of Rockingham.

In 1778, Keppel, sailing in HMS Victory, led the British fleet against the French at the Battle of Ushant. Both fleets manoeuvred around each other for days but the battle only lasted a few minutes and only one broadside was fired.

He was tried for cowardice afterwards but was honourably acquitted when it transpired Sir Hugh Palliser, one of Keppel's admirals had failed to carry out his orders. Keppel then went on to become First Lord of the Admiralty. The Marquis of Rockingham supported his friend throughout his trial and shortly after his acquittal in 1778, started work on building Keppel's Column at Kimberworth in honour of his excellent naval career and naval glories for England.

The Fourth Earl, also William Keppel's son, was the Lord Thomas Keppel of Abermarle and his granddaughter was Marianne Eva North, Robert Charles Otter's new wife. They kept Royal scandal in the family in that Marianne's cousin, Alice Edmonstone Keppel, who was born in 1869, was the famous mistress of King Edward VII.

Marianne Eva North was named after her famous aunt, the renowned artist, Marianne North. She was her father's sister and she was classed as one of the finest artists of horticulture that had ever lived. She travelled all over the world, making sketches as she went. The sketches were turned into magnificent paintings. There is a special section of Kew Gardens in London being the Marianne North Gallery, where there are details of her life and works, which are also on display (832 separate paintings).

After their marriage, Robert Charles and Marianne Eva resided at Edwinstowe Hall in Edwinstowe, Nottinghamshire (not too far from the Clayworth Estate) and lived there along with five servants being two housemaids, one lady's maid, cook and footman.

Swinton Hall's tenant, Major Edward Bowen Cooke died aged 51, on 11 August 1877. His widow and children, probably for economic reasons, then left the Hall. In the same year, it appears Jonathan White also left, leaving the Hall and grounds empty once more.

Swinton was, at this time, overseen by a local board made up from the community. The initiative to form these local boards nationally was from an Act of Parliament dating back to 1876. Funding for the boards was collected from local rate payers.

By 1878, the growing town of Swinton was experiencing water shortages and a quick solution was needed. Henry Otter was approached by the then New Swinton Local Board to see it he would allow them to pump water from an old coal mining shaft situated in Brookfield, which was part of the Swinton Estate lands. The water sample proved to be of good quality and so Henry started supplying the town with water to put them on. In the following two years, the Town sunk more wells to alleviate the problems. Unfortunately, good relations with the Board did not continue in the future.

During 1879 at the age of 28, Henry's daughter Constance Otter married Erasmus Wilkinson but this was to be a wedding out of the area. Erasmus was a man of the cloth with a devotion to duty and a determination to travel. Erasmus was born in November 1845 at Marlborough, Wiltshire. He was the son of the late Reverend Matthew Wilkinson and his wife, Latitia. He had previously been the Vicar of Melksham in Wiltshire and a Canon of Salisbury Cathedral.

He was schooled privately, finally obtaining an MA at Oxford University. By 1871, he was a classics master, teaching up and coming scholars. He had deep religious convictions, with a desire to help anyone. The wedding took place at St Marleybone Church, London. The Church had hit the news in 1846 when poet, Robert Browning, secretly married Elizabeth Barret after a scandalous elopement from her strict family home. It makes one wonder if perhaps there was somewhat of a repetition by the new couple of some of this. Why didn't they marry at the bride's local Church or even Clayworth? The announcements in the press simply anote the event and refer to the fact she was the daughter of Henry Otter, gentleman of Swinton House. This was untypical and does make one wonder. After the wedding, the couple moved to Bristol, where Erasmus had taken a teaching post.

In the Minutes of the Local Board, dated 18 October 1880, it was noted a long debate took place regarding the state of the wall making up the road frontage at Swinton House. The clerk (Mr F L Harrop) was instructed to serve a seven day repair notice, demanding the repair of the wall and stating that Henry is responsible for compensation to anyone who is injured by falling stones. This is not the wall you see today as this wall was moved back from the original position when Fitzwilliam Street was widened. Presumably, Henry completed this task as on photographs taken some years later, the wall looks to be of sound structure.

A new tenant was found for Swinton Hall, moving in during 1880. He was Edward Barker, his wife Ellen and their only son, Edward and two servants, Annie and Agnes Bond. Edward was the youngest son of Samuel Barker (deceased), iron founder, industrialist and owner of the Don Pottery. Edward himself was born at Mexborough in 1844 and his wife was born at Leominster in 1849.

At the young age of 21, Edward had acquired one third equity of the Don Pottery business. This was back in 1865. Under his father's will, he inherited an option to purchase the one-third share in the Don Pottery and he exercised it.

Following the death of his brothers, Peter and Henry, Edward then continued the business on as a sole trader. The Don Pottery had been established as a business since 1801 and his father, Samuel, bought the factory in 1839.

The 1881 census states Edward's occupation as "earthenware manufacturer and employer of one hundred and ninety one persons". During the year, Edward put the pottery up for sale at a price of £12000 but there were no takers. Instead, he agreed to rent out the works to Messrs John Adamson of Swinton, earthenware manufacturer, John Wilkinson of Swinton, glass bottle manufacturer, Charles Scorah of Mexborough, butcher and Edward Thomas Smith of Mexborough, bankers clerk.

The Rotherham and Masbro Advertiser ran the story:-

The Don Pottery, Swinton. These works, which have been partially closed for some weeks, are to be re-opened. The Pottery has, for many years, been carried on by Messrs Samuel Barker and son and latterly by Edward Barker alone and that gentleman is now retiring. It was feared that the works would be standing for some considerable time. But four gentlemen in the neighbourhood have now taken on a long lease and work will resume about the middle of the present month. The old works people, many of whom will probably be re-engaged, expressed the greatest satisfaction that the work is to be resumed.

The actual sale terms were an annual rent of £350 rising to £450. The sale of the tools and loose plant for £2000 and granting an option to purchase the freehold of the site for £8900 and lastly, assigning the right to continue using the name, Samuel Barker and Son.

The 1881 census for Swinton House records the following:-

NAME	AGE	POSITION	BIRTH PLACE
Henry Otter	73	Head	Clayworth, Notts
Mary Otter	56	Wife	Bath, Somerset
Alice M Otter	32	Daughter	Tickhill, Yorks
Catherine Otter	25	Daughter	Swinton, Yorks
Isobel L Otter	22	Daughter	Swinton, Yorks
Ellen Edwards	25	Servant	Cardington, Shropshire
Hannah E Newton	26	Servant	Gt Peatling, Leicester
Mary Knowles	26	Servant	South Muskham, Notts
Mary Morgan	16	Servant	Whitehaven, Cumberland

On the day of the census, Ann Otter was visiting her cousin, Robert Henry Otter, solicitor and attorney, and was staying at his residence at St Leonard's, Hastings along with three servants.

Interestingly, in addition to Edward Barker living in the Hall, also recorded as living within the grounds of Swinton Hall were:-

NAME	AGE	POSITION	BIRTH PLACE
George Smith	-	Coachman	Barmbrough, York
Sarah E Smith	34	Wife	Kilnhurst, York

They were obviously working for Edward Barker.

Life continued on at Swinton House but then, tragedy struck when Henry Otter's beloved wife, Mary, died on 4 September 1881. She died on a Sunday evening after a short illness. She had been a Swinton resident for 30 years. The South Yorkshire Times commented, "She had endeared herself to the needy of the area by her unostentatious charity and urbanity and her demise will be greatly felt. So few of the well-to-do nowadays take pity on those whose circumstances are not so fortunate and when they are called to the better world, they leave a gap, which is not easily filled". Henry was very close to Mary and her death was obviously devastating to him. He had her body transported to Clayworth on the following Wednesday and a service was held there at St Peter's Church before burying her within the Otter family plots. So again, it was back to the true Otter headquarters, with no burial at Swinton or Wath.

It was at this time that Henry obviously engaged himself in deep thought. Half of his eight children were married but he still had some daughters who were unmarried and had to think of the future of the Swinton Estate. Alice, aged 32, Catherine, aged 25 and Isabel, aged 22 and Anne, aged 18, were all still in residence at Swinton House.

In 1881, Henry entered into a further lease with Charlesworth's for more coal extraction from the Swinton lands. He was still building income from the coal mines and would now receive a further annual rent and an extra royalty per ton. It was around this time that Henry instructed a Joseph Aquilla Bower to build some more cottages on the left hand side of Temperance Street, so boosting the rental income further. This income was to an estate whose future was still not settled in Henry's own mind. To this end, he consulted the long standing Wath solicitors, Nicholson's and listened to their advice regarding securing the future.

On 4 March 1882 he made a will. The will made the following provisions. He considered that his two married daughters, Barbara and Constance, would be looked after by their husbands on the basis that he had made very generous dowries when they were married. Bearing in mind the earlier comments regarding Constance, Henry may not have been one hundred percent behind the marriage but he was a good father and had not shown any chastisement.

On his death, his four unmarried daughters were to be awarded £160 per annum, payable half yearly each from the Estate income until such time that they were married when they would be awarded £1000 each but then the income from the Estate would stop. He also insisted Swinton House and all its furnishings had to be left for the use of his unmarried daughters whilst ever they required it – rent free of course. All they had to do was keep it insured.

Apart from these requests, the rest of the Estate went to his son and heir, Robert Charles who was now immersed in his army career. He made son Robert and the former Swinton trustees, R J Pettiward and E Brookbank executors. The Will was witnessed by Thomas Reeder, Solicitor, and by Thomas Humphreys, his clerk.

Henry obviously went away and re-thought the situation as he returned back on 4 March to the solicitors to make an alteration (codicil). On his death, he wanted to pay out the legacy of £200 cash to each of his three unmarried daughters and £50 each to his married daughters in order to give them immediate access to funds.

The daughters were not without some wealth themselves. Catherine Otter held land herself in Wath and she granted a 22 year mining lease to Charlesworth's in her own name. This land may originate from the old Jackson farmland holdings.

By 1882, Henry's health was on the wane. He had not enjoyed any degree of fitness for several years and had frequently been attended by his relative, Doctor Blythman. Since the death of his wife, he had started to noticeably deteriorate. It was reported he lived a very quiet life even though he was a hardened conservative and convinced churchman. Perhaps he was becoming a little more cantankerous?

By 1883, there was growing evidence that Henry was in conflict with the local board. Very hot on the agenda at every board meeting was the subject of the water supply and development of a bigger network to meet the demands.

Correspondence was sent to Henry regarding pollution found in his well in Cliffield. They were concerned that someone would be made ill and warned him that he would be liable personally for any damages arising and this would not be paid by the rate payers. He was ordered to clean up his act.

This would have really aggravated Henry. History shows that these first local boards suffered from attacks by providers of the law, landowners and industrialists. Henry was in two of these classes. As a provider of the law, he was used to people being imposed on by him, not the other way round. Also, as a wealthy landowner, he thought he should be allowed to run his own affairs without interference from a local board. The members of the board were farmers and tradesmen – middle classes "Petty Bourgiousie". Henry most definitely thought he was superior to them.

As Henry owned so much land and had prosperity, it would have been inevitable he would often come up in despatches.

Henry's response to the board's letter was to go to the top. He wrote to the head of the National Body of Government Boards. They, in turn, wrote to Frederick Lee Harrop as clerk of the board. Henry's letter had not only complained of their impertinence but made allegations about their non-production of accounting information as regards the Parish award and expenditures.

The clerk was instructed to reply at once to the effect of what the National Award had been and to state the records had always been available and could be inspected without difficulty.

Frederick Lee Harrop was a seasoned solicitor and would not have slipped up on a basic requirement, so leaving the board and himself as their legal advisor, wide open.

Henry's complaint was vexatious and as it was completely unfounded, probably made him look a little amateur – not his usual style.

More sadness came to Swinton House in 1884. Daughter Constance and her husband, Erasmus Wilkinson, had travelled to Valparaiso in South America and were residing there. He had finished his teaching post in Bristol and was struck by the spirit of adventure. He was working as a missionary for the Church. In 1865, religious freedom in Chile was granted and 1875 saw the establishment of the First Anglican Church. There was a band of volunteers who went out to administer religion to the Chileans including Erasmus and Constance. They had two children, Henry Matthew, born in 1883 and Frederick Charles, born in 1884. Tragedy came when Constance died on 28 February, aged 34. She died either during childbirth or shortly after. Despite the children being young in the interim, Erasmus continued with his missionary work, living at Villa Constitution in the Republic of Argentina. It is not known if her body was brought back but probably not as she would have most likely been interred at Clayworth where she isn't.

In 1885, Edward Barker left Swinton Hall moving to 64 Belsize Road, Hampstead, London. He finally ended up living in Devon, where he died in 1919.

A new tenant for the Hall, a Mrs Rachel Barber, was found. She was born on 16 December 1809, the daughter of a wealthy family who lived at Whorton Grange near Darlington. She married Milah Barber, a colliery owner of Kimberworth House, Kimberworth, Rotherham. She had two daughters, Elizabeth born in 1834 and Mary, who was born much later in 1848. Her husband's family originated from the Attercliffe area and had built up a substantial mining business, trading then as "Brown Brothers".

On the death of her husband, she continued to oversee the colliery business, employing 85 men. Her eldest daughter in the meantime, married the then up and coming young solicitor from Swinton, called Frederick Lee Harrop (the same person previously mentioned as Clerk Advisor to the Local Board). Around 1869, Frederick Lee moved to Highfield House on Fitzwilliam Street (the old SUDC offices). By 1871, the Barber colliery business was winding down and Rachel and her unmarried daughter, Mary, moved to Cliff House on Station Street. She lived there on independent means with servants. She was noted for her generosity and benevolence.

Following the departure of Edward Barker from Swinton Hall, she decided to take up the tenancy. Bearing in mind the proximity of Highfield House to Swinton hall, she was only one hundred yards from her daughter and her husband, Lawyer Harrop.

The start of 1886 saw Robert Otter promoted to the rank of Lieutenant with the Sherwood Foresters and more family celebrations were to come.

In the first week of May 1886, Henry's daughter, Isabella Otter married Mr Leonard Swain Mortlock Marsh, the wedding strangely taking place in the New Forest. He was born in 1858 at Tuxford, Nottinghamshire. He was the third son of six children born to the Reverend Henry Augustus Marsh and his wife, Eliza. They all resided at No 3 Lincoln Street together with two live in servants. Leonard trained to be a civil engineer, travelling to different areas to carry out his profession. In 1881, he was living at Ecclesall Bierlow, Sheffield, in a boarding house together with two other gentlemen from Tuxford with him, being the engineer for the Sheffield Water Corporation.

On the evening before the wedding, Henry entertained the tenants of the Swinton Estate with a special tea at Swinton House and entertainment was provided. Henry was not in good health and could not undertake the journey to the New Forest and so hosted the home celebrations. The tenants left several presents for the couple as also did the house servants. I would imagine Henry greatly missed the input of his wife with all this.

Isabella was staying with Robert Eyre (her cousin) at his manor house at Bartley Grange, Metley Marsh in Hampshire and many guests travelled down from Swinton and Clayworth to witness the event on the day of the wedding. However, plans had to be changed. Robert C Otter was (in his father's absence) to give his sister away. A telegram arrived however, from Eaton Hall only hours before confirming he would not be there as his wife was too ill to travel. At the last hour, Robert Eyre himself volunteered to walk her down the aisle. Her sister, Alice and cousin, Miss Eyre, were bridesmaids. The wedding ceremony was performed by the groom's father, Reverend H Marsh and the groom's brother was best man.

As they left the Church for the short walk back to the carriage, the path was adorned with wild flowers picked by the local school children. Several of the Grange's staff, in new uniforms, lined the path to keep it clear as there were a lot of onlookers and well-wishers there. The guests all returned to the Grange for a late breakfast. The couple then left for honeymoon. I do find it odd that only one sister was bridesmaid. The wedding guests included the Warde-Aldams of Frickley, the Fullertons of Thrybergh and Sir John Tilly, KCB. Details of the bride's outfit worn on the day are as follows:-

"She wore a rich but simple dress of white brocade satin with bodice and train of Ottoman silk trimmed with old lace, a small wreath of orange blossom and veil fastened with diamond pins. She carried an exquisite bouquet, the gift of the grooms. The bridesmaids' dresses were of cream Arabian cotton trimmed with lace bows, shoes and gloves to match, cream lace bonnets and each carried beautiful bouquets of white and pink tinted flowers."

Please see appendices for a full list of wedding gifts.

Leonard and Isabella started married life taking the tenancy of the Manor House at Hooton Roberts complete with three live in servants. Isabel's unmarried sister, Alice Mary Otter, also moved in with them. It is believed it would have been Isabella's wealth that enabled the new couple to take on this commitment.

The close of 1886 saw Henry's health deteriorate even further and sadly, on 12 August 1887, Henry Otter died and with him went the Otter solidity of Swinton so desperately wanted earlier by his family at Clayworth. His funeral took place the following Sunday when his coffin, which was made by Mr Baxter of Swinton, was conveyed by Mr Biggins of Mexborough by carriage from Swinton House to Clayworth back to the Otter Headquarters. It reached there at 10.00pm on the Saturday evening. His coffin was placed in the centre isle of Clayworth Church and his funeral took place early at 8.00am Sunday morning. The coffin

The Earl of Strafford at Hooton Roberts, which was formerly the home of Anne Otter and Lucy Otter.

was born to the graveside by the deceased's servants and tenants of the Clayworth Estate. The vault in which lay the remains of his deceased wife was opened and dressed in ferns and flowers and Henry's body was lain into it. The last solemn rights from the Church of England were performed by Reverend H Jubb. A funeral breakfast, very common in Victorian times, was held at Clayworth Hall afterwards. It was the end of an era. A newspaper report at the time quotes that Henry owned several estates at the time of his death. A lot of his estate had been placed into family Trusts, which meant it would not appear for taxation purposes. The value of the Estate, still in his own name, was some £6165 6s 9d. It was believed to be substantially understated for taxation purposes.

Rachel Barber's tenancy at the Hall was not long as she died on 20 August 1887. She had enjoyed good health but was then stricken and her illness was very short. According to Rachel's wishes, she was interred at St Margaret's Churchyard in the Harrop family plot so that eventually, her daughter and son-in-law could join her. It was noted that in the mourners at her funeral were Catherine and Alice Otter and her relatives from Darlington, who were residing at Wycliffe Hall.

TRUST BENEFACTOR –
ROBERT CHARLES OTTER ERA

This now meant that Swinton born Robert Charles Otter was the new owner of the Estate lands and Swinton Hall and Swinton House. He had already amassed some wealth himself through marriage and had enjoyed other family inheritances from both sides.

As a memorial to the Otters of Swinton, Henry's daughters organised a memorial centre light to be inserted in the Church's east window. This is the only reference found anywhere to the Otters in Swinton's Church!

The Swinton properties were not to be used for long by the Otters following the death of Henry. Swinton House would also eventually be tenanted out. The Otter occupation at Swinton was nearly at an end. Catherine Otter moved away to live in Chislehurst, Kent, so leaving Swinton House with only Ann remaining. Ann initially moved into the vacant Swinton Hall but later moved out and took up residence in Hooton Roberts so being nearer to Isabella and her other sister, Alice.

As Robert Charles took stock of his inheritance and its implications, he was not comfortable regarding his commitment to pay the annual annuities out to his unmarried sisters. Robert decided to take legal action to try and alter the terms and conditions of his father's will. First though,

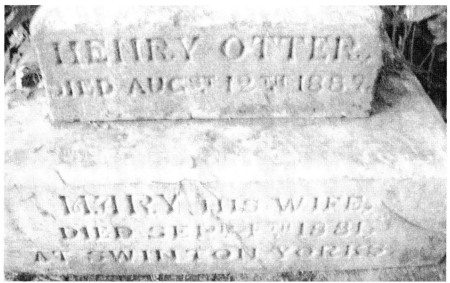

Headstone of Henry Otter and Mary, his wife, situated at St Peter's Churchyard, Clayworth.

he had to obtain probate. On 10 April 1888, Robert appeared alone in the Probate Division Court at Wakefield Registry to obtain the Will's probate. The other two executors both resigned their positions, leaving Robert alone to handle the matter.

On 14 April 1888, solicitors were engaged and Robert's application was heard at the High Court of Justice. The parties cited to the action were Robert Otter versus all his sisters, himself and his wife. He sought permission from the Court to have the Swinton Estate valued, put into eight shares providing one share each for him and his wife and one share each to his six sisters. He then proposed to make a cash award to each of his sisters of the total amount of their worth in return for freeing from all the Wills' obligations, etc, and it would leave the Swinton Estate intact.

This action, in reality, was very generous by Robert as he was also bringing back into the inheritance his sisters and his deceased sister's children, some of whom, due to their being married, had been left out of the will by their father.

The High Court of Justice found for the proposed changes in the terms and conditions of the will. It was decided that the dead should not be able to dictate to the living, well, not for many years. Robert paid each of his sisters' £3179.40 each.

This meant that the value of the Estate at Swinton and Wath in 1888 was £25,432 (bear in mind the valuation for tax given as only £6,165 at Henry's death. This would evaluate to £11,355,880 at 2006 prices when considering present day values of building and agricultural land).

So, life now continued at Swinton but the Estate is now just a rent roll.

Henry's daughter Barbara was, in 1888, widowed when the Reverend Alfred William Wickham Davies, her husband, died. She continued to live in Halifax.

In 1890, the youngest of Henry's daughters, Ann, was married to Mr Herbert St John Durnford, gentleman. He was born in 1860, the youngest of eight brothers and also having four sisters. He was born at Eton College where his father, Reverend Francis Edward Durnford was, at the time, a lower house master in Holy Orders. They all lived within the college. He was educated at first by a governess and then at Eton itself. He then went on to study mining engineering. He travelled to Yorkshire to work with the Fitzwilliam mines, lodging at Birdwell and ending up as the Earl's mining agent, overseeing all the colliery interests. He qualified as a member of the Institute of Civil Engineers. It is presumably whilst he was working in South Yorkshire that he met Ann Otter.

Ann was determined to participate in what would be seen as a fashionable wedding. She did not use St Margaret's Church but decided to use the Church of Hooton Roberts, this being where she now resided. It is noted that there was a large number of onlookers who had come from Swinton, Kilnhurst, Thrybergh and Mexborough. The Church was beautifully decorated out with floral and fruit arrangements. The clergymen who participated in the ceremony was the Reverend W W Dodsworth of Chislehurst, Kent and the Reverend Robert Routh of Longstock, Hampshire.

The bridesmaids were Eva Mary Otter (brother Robert Charles' daughter), Dorothy Otter, Edwyna Durnford and Muriel Leigh Bennett. The pages were Masters R J Otter and Ivor Gatty. Mr A W Drury acted as groomsman.

After the ceremony, the wedding guests moved next door to the Manor House, where her sister lived (now the Earl of Strafford Public House). An awning was stretched out to cover the route from the Church porch to the entrance of the Hall under which was a crimson carpet. The whole route was strewn with flowers. A string band (John Pecks) struck up into music as the bride and groom appeared. A photographer, Mr Cherrington of Swinton, took photos of the event. I wonder where these are today.

In addition to family members, the wedding guests included:-

Captain and Mrs J Durnford, R.N, Captain and Mrs Godfrey Armitage, Reverend Harworth, Reverend Brewin, Dr C Blythman, Reverend T Beard, Mrs Bowen Cooke,

Dr Clarke, Reverend Ellershaw (Mexborough), Reverend Faber, Reverend Houghton, Reverend Levett (Swinton), Canon Leigh Bennett, Reverend MacNaughton, Sir William and Lady Mahon, Reverend Partington, Reverend H Sheppard (Kilnhurst), Sir John and Lady Weston, Canon Wright, Mrs Cooke-Yarborough (Campsall Hall).

The longer serving servants were transported to the Church in a wagonette to witness the wedding. Afterwards, they were transported to Conisbrough, where they were treated to tea and ale. Gifts were received from the attendees and also the Bishop of Chichester, the Archdeacon Reverend W Bland, Mrs Francis Terry, the servants at Hooton Roberts, Mrs Warde-Aldham, Reverend Stevens, Lady Deaton,

Reverend Pym, Reverend Heap, Dr Pescott-Roberts and Admiral Douglas.

Details of the bride's dress were described as follows:-

"The bride was beautifully attired in white corded silk with a veil fastened by diamond pearls, the gift of the bridegroom."

(Please see appendices for a full list of wedding gifts.)

As the town continued to expand, so had the network of utility pipes in a growing underground network. The board meeting of 18 July 1890 acknowledged that they had to pay way leave compensation to Mr White of £5, to Mr Otter of £12 and Mr E T Harrop of £24.

Robert Charles moved from Edwinstowe back to Royston Manor, Clayworth in 1891 and remained there in residence.

A tenant was also found for Swinton House, Augustus James Fenner. He was born in 1864 at Greenwich, Kent, the son of Henry and Elizabeth Fenner. He was sent to boarding school in Market Rasen and then went on to be a trained as an industrial chemist. In 1890, he married Florence, the daughter of Guy Senior at Barnsley. Guy Senior and his brother had started the Oakwell Brewery in 1858. Their father had been a brewer in

Aerial view of Swinton, in which Swinton House and Swinton Hall can just be made out towards the bottom right hand half of the picture.

Huddersfield so they were very familiar with the trade.

Brother Paul died in 1867 and Guy continued alone. Initially, after their marriage, the newlyweds lived at the Senior family home, Beever Hall, situated on Pontefract Road, Barnsley. It does conjure the question whether Augustus Fenner met his wife whilst working for the Oakwell Brewery.

When Swinton House became vacant, they jumped at the chance of occupancy. By this time, the Oakwell Brewery owned some eighty six public houses locally. These included Station Inn at Kilnhurst, the Prince of Wales and Park Hotel at Mexborough. The company continued on until 1961 when it was taken over by John Smith's by which time, it had acquired a further eighty seven licensed properties, including The Harlington Inn, Manvers Arms at Adwick upon Dearne and Canal Tavern, Swinton.

A new tenant for Swinton Hall was also found. James White, came from a long line of millers. He was classed as one of the leading millers of Yorkshire. He originated from Wath and was born in 1830. His wife, Elizabeth, was born in 1836, hailing from Methley, Leeds. He was accredited with owning around 180 acres of farmland around Adwick and employed up to eleven men and two boys in addition to the milling activity. When he was a young man, his father had, for a time, tenanted part of Swinton Hall outbuildings, but this time, he was back tenanting the whole Hall. James White lived at the Hall with son, Frederick (who worked for his father) and unmarried daughters Florence, Lucy and Elizabeth along with three live-in servants.

The Don Corn Mill was founded by him in 1884. The only system known of milling up to this time was that of using the stone system. For his new mill, he built a system of rollers that ground the corn speedily. It also sifted, dried and purified it. He was quite an industrial innovator and obviously enjoying success. After James retired, son Frederick, aged 27, took over the running of the business. It is recorded that the White's had left Swinton Hall by 1892. The daughters were still all unmarried and in their twenties. They moved to Christchurch in Doncaster. So another short tenancy had come to an end but now an Otter was about to return.

Incidentally, 1892 brought national concerns to infectious disease and each town had to make available a place of isolation for the infected to be housed, away from the main population. Robert Otter responded by offering a site for the town to use. His letter was unsolicited. The Council did not take up his offer and instead, made plans to use the Waterloo Kiln on the old Rockingham Pottery site. This was the cheapest option for them as it would mean adapting costs only compared to new construction.

Isabel Marsh, Robert's sister and her husband, moved back to Swinton from the Manor House, Hooton Roberts into the vacant Swinton Hall. An "Otter" was now, for the last time, in residence.

Her husband had joined the Conservative Party and was trying to get more involved in the community. An opportunity arose in the summer of 1894 when there developed a crisis in the funding of the National School at Kilnhurst and Isobel saw an angle.

Nationally, the Church of England had established 6000 new schools but they needed volunteers and charitable assistance to continue. Some £600000 nationally had to be realised each year. To this end, it was decided to form an "Exhibition and Conversazione" in the Kilnhurst School. The idea was that the gentry of the area would loan interesting artefacts to be displayed and the public would pay to file by and see these.

Isobel and her sister, Alice, loaned them some artefacts of Admiral Lord Nelson's that they had housed in the Hall. These included a carved figure of him (done by one of his officers) that was originally part of the flagship "The Victory", some of Nelson's autographed letters and other memorabilia including the banner placed on his coffin, a gun from the ship and Nelson's prayer book. They also loaned a set of Roman coins, a letter from David Livingstone and one from Oliver Cromwell. It is believed these items had been purchased from the Gatty family originally.

They also loaned, for display, a carved tomahawk and other weapons of the South Sea Islands, a Marabou priest's hat and an old black sack from medieval times.

Other artefacts were borrowed from the Blunn's (Kilnhurst Glass Works), T B Bosville (Ravenfield Park), Reverened Levett (Swinton), Joel Kirby (Mexborough Benefactor) and The Glasby's (Kilnhurst sculptor). A star attraction was a phonograph with fourteen ear tubes that would have allowed selected listeners to hear the music record sent over specially by the Edison-Bell Corporation. The event was a terrific success.

The Local Government Act 1894 saw the creation of the Swinton Urban and District Council. Leonard Swain Mortlock Marsh put himself forth as a candidate. This was not easy in that many of the old Swinton Board (the predecessor to the Council) members were also standing. Despite the threat, he was successfully elected with the second highest votes.

In the South Yorkshire Times of 14 December 1894, he set out his manifesto. He was the only one of all the candidates to do any real electioneering. He referred to his twenty years experience of overseeing engineering projects as being valuable to push for "a good water supply and a thorough system of sewerage for every house in the town". These, he said, "are recognised as the necessities of modern well being". He wanted to provide allotments for those who wanted them at reasonable rents. He wanted to lobby the Government to payout pensions to the elderly without the drawbacks of a lack of self respect in proving the need. He wished to light up all public thoroughfares throughout the town. His electioneering paid off as he polled such high votes.

The candidate with the highest votes became the first leader of SUDC. This was Conservative Joseph Aquilla Bower. The South Yorkshire Times reported no-one in the district could lay greater claim to such a position. In the past, he had shown much wisdom and good judgement and his position of chairman is unquestionable. The results of the election were as follows:-

ELECTED			NOT ELECTED		
J A Bower	Con	698*	T Hattersley	Con	305*
LSM Marsh	Con	549	J Sharpley	Con	300*
L Charlesworth	Lab	532*	Robert Maiden	Lab	299
Enoch Jagger	L	434*	James Bell	Lab	259
T Whitfield	Lab	418*	N Noble	L	234*
W Annables	Lab	405	C Phillipson	Con	229
C Hattersley	Con	393*	Joshua Walker	Con	196
W Cornwall	Lab	392			
Thomas Hart	Lab	369			
J Goodinson	L	344*			
T Dutchman	L	335*			
W Phillips	Lab	324			

(* = members of old board)

It was reported in the South Yorkshire Times afterwards that very few meetings were held by candidates with only Mr Marsh taking the real initiative. There were three polling stations, one on Bridge Street, one at the old Board Offices and one at Kilnhurst. The election returning officer was town solicitor, Mr F L Harrop. Unfortunately, any election sense of triumph was short lived for within a week of being elected, tragedy again came to the Otter family on 20 December 1894. Shortly after the birth of her son, Jack, Isobel Lucy died, aged 35. Her death came suddenly and unexpectedly. Her obituary notice confirmed her generous nature and that she was a benefactor to the poor of the parish. The Council passed an official vote of condolence and offered Mr Marsh time off from his duties.

Mr Baxter, undertaker of Swinton, arranged for Isobel's body to be carried back to Clayworth (the Otter headquarters) for burial. Mr Biggins of Mexborough provided the carriage. A terrific gale blew all that day and the journey was treacherous. Her funeral took place on the Sunday morning.

Following Isobel's death, Mr Marsh, along with his young son, Jack and Alice Mary Otter, his wife's sister, moved to Birley House, Ecclesfield, Sheffield. Swinton probably held too many bad memories. Whilst it seemed strange for Alice to be with Mr Marsh, she had lived with them after they were married and probably acted as a nursemaid to Isobel's child, Jack. She later married Mr Marsh, becoming his second wife.

1894 also saw Robert consolidate his father's two old leases with Charlesworth's for coal extraction into a new lease. The new lease was also for thirty five years and was for an annual rent of £367.10 plus royalties per ton of coal extracted.

Robert also sold some Swinton land to Andrew Merryweather (estate agent of Whiston) who proceeded to negotiate his own lease for the mineral rights of the Barnsley bed. The Estate was slowly being chipped away.

Following the Marsh's departure, a new tenant was found for Swinton Hall. He was John Grayson Lowood. He was born at Bolsterstone in Derbyshire in 1835. His parents had resided at Spink Hall where he was born. His father was William Lowood and his mother was Mary Grayson. His mother's family had considerable status and that is why young John was given a double-barrelled surname. It often occurred in such situations and helped to secure inheritances from both sides of the family, which, in his case, later in life, it worked. John had been involved in the mining industry and had prospered himself.

He owned the former chemistry works at Deepcar, where he operated a ganister mine and refractory, producing a variety of bricks. He also operated a coal mine at Lowood, Wharncliffe and another at Stannington, Sheffield. He had married his first wife, Ada Matilda in 1860 and had two daughters, Florence, born in 1865 and Georgina Lillian, born in 1869, living at Five

Swinton Hall, taken from Fitzwilliam Street, believed to be around 1900. The lady in the picture is thought to be Martha Anne Lowood, the wife of John Grayson Lowood, the occupant of the Hall at the time. Their youngest child was born in 1894.

Oaks, 421 Glossop Road, Sheffield. His first wife died and he then re-married, starting another family somewhat late in life. He inherited the Firestone Quarry from his uncle, John Grayson, which was at Attercliffe, Sheffield. He also tried to become the elected representative on the Sheffield Council in 1891 but failed. He re-tried in 1893 and, this time, was successful. Shortly afterwards, he decided to retire and sold off all his interests and moved into Swinton. At first, he was living at "Thornleigh" on Station Street, which he sold. Then, in the summer of 1894, he moved into Swinton Hall with his second wife Martha Ann, whom he wed in 1891, and three young children, daughters Ida and Gladys and son John, who were born between 1892 and 1894. He was aged 57 when the first of his second family was born. He lived at Swinton Hall along with his widowed sister, Ann, and a parlour maid, a housemaid, a children's nurse, a cook, a housekeeper and a coachman. His sister moved in after the premature death of his second wife shortly after moving to the Hall. His tenancy at Swinton Hall came to a sudden end on 1 August 1902 when he died unexpectedly. His funeral was carried out by Butterfield's. His coffin was carried by horse-drawn hearse to Swinton Station and then transported by train to Sheffield where, by his own instructions, he was to be buried. His sister and his children then left.

Another tenant for Swinton House was also found following the departure of the Fenners, with a lease being given to a Henry Pearson. It is believed the Fenners moved away to settle in Ilkley. There never seemed to be a shortage of tenants for either of the grand properties so providing good rental income.

Robert Otter's military career continued and by 1895, he was made Captain in Command. In 1897, he was appointed as Aide-de-Campe to Brigadier General Viscount Newark (Earl of Manvers). On retiring from the regiment, he was made an honorary rank of Lieutenant Colonel. Like his father, he became a magistrate at the Retford Courts and also became a tax commissioner.

Also, like his father, he became involved in public work, becoming a member of the River Idle Drainage Commission, eventually becoming Chairman. He was also one of the first members of Retford Rural District Council where he served for some eleven years. His love of horses and hunting continued throughout his life and he was Joint Master of the West Norfolk Hounds and acted as honorary secretary to Viscount Galway's hunt. But for thirteen years, he acted as deputy master to none other than his land owning neighbour to the Swinton Estate, Earl Fitzwilliam's Grove Hounds Hunt. Some controversy surrounded fox hunting even back then but in reply to a letter in the Retford Times, he stated "Foxing hunting was good as it also helped provide the right kind of horses for the British Army". Whilst at Clayworth, he bred and maintained his own pack of Beagles.

Robert Charles Otter and his wife had six children in all. Of his children, one of his sons, also called Robert John Charles, became Captain of the Norfolk Regiment. He saw action as a signalling officer in the South African Boer War, being badly wounded in 1901. He continued to serve in South

Robert John Charles Otter, here seen seated with his dog, acted as signalling officer in the South African Boer War before being badly wounded in 1901. He was killed during the early part of the first World War.

Africa with the 6th Mounted Infantry and remained out there until 1908, being involved in the suppressing of the Guerilla campaign. He served in India between 1911 and 1914. He was married in 1914 to Gwendoline Bernere. He became one of the "old contemptibles" but was killed in action on the battlefield on 15 February 1915 aged 34 and was buried in the churchyard at Dranouter, France.

Another of Robert Charles' sons, Robin Otter, became a Lieutenant Colonel, MC and served with the 5th London Regiment. He was married to Mary Laura Troutbridge on 21 February 1916 who was the daughter of Admiral Ernest Chance Thomas Troutbridge. They went on to have four daughters. He had first become a commissioned officer in 1906 and had rose up the ranks to Lieutenant by 1909. In line with family tradition, he was also attached to the Norfolk Regiment. He was wounded several times during the First World War. Another son, Henry Royston Otter, became mid-shipman in the Royal Navy. He was accidentally killed whilst carrying out revolver practice whilst home on leave on 27 November 1909.

The fourth son was Anthony who took his religious beliefs right to the top, serving as the Bishop of Grantham. Daughter, Eva Mary, married Sir Lovelace Stamer, 4th Baronet. In the publication "The Plantagenet Roll of Royal Blood – The Clarence Volume", the Otter family children are listed as descendants of monarchy.

Early minutes of SUDC show that Robert Charles started selling off more land from the Swinton Estate. He sold the sites of Cliffield Road and Temperance Street for housing development. The latter was bought by Joseph Aquilla Bower.

The constant water distribution problems that plagued the town resurrected themselves once more. The water pressure needed to be increased by the building of a water tower. Robert sold them a plot for £75 near the Woodman

Lady Eva Mary Stamer, daughter of Robert Charles Otter and Marianne Eva who married Sir Lovelace Stamer, the Fourth Baronet.

end of the town. This land is still corporation owned today. Around the site, there were messy coal outcrops as Robert had previously sold extraction licenses to individuals. This came as a bit of a nuisance as when the Council bought some more land in that vicinity, it needed small shafts to be tidied up and the land surface re-landscaping.

The council had had to pay compensation to Robert Otter several times in the 1890's for having to cross certain pieces of land with underground pipes.

SWINTON HALL -
THE JOSEPH AQUILLA-BOWER ERA

In a letter dated December 1903 from Mr Turner, founder of South Yorkshire Times written from his address at The Beeches, on Fitzwilliam Street, Swinton, it refers to the fact that Mr Joseph Aquilla Bower had just bought Thornleigh on Station Street from Mr J G Lowood who had been the tenant at Swinton Hall but was now deceased. Thornleigh was a very impressive property in its own right but the opportunity of moving into Swinton Hall after Mr Lowood's death obviously appealed more to Joseph.

Joseph was born in Swinton in 1851. He was one of six children. His father was Charles (born in 1825) and mother, Elizabeth (born in 1823). They lived firstly at 54 Church Street but shortly afterwards moved to 28 Pottery Lane. Charles was a builder, employing a couple of men and later, he incorporated some of his sons to come and work alongside him. He had traded profitably and acquired land and property himself during his business years.

When Joseph Aquilla left school, he first trained to be a stone mason,

The former home of Joseph Aquilla Bower is in use by Rotherham Metropolitan Borough Council today.

Grounds of Swinton Hall during the time of Joseph Aquilla Bower. The grounds were kept in immaculate condition.

influenced no doubt by his father. He showed great aspirations and decided to change direction. He gained employment in the offices of the Wentworth Estates. Here the Sixth Earl Fitzwilliam's Estate, containing many hundreds of properties and owned land were all managed. Joseph trained to be an architect. He later married Anne Elizabeth Rhodes who was born in 1857 and originated from Staincross and they lived at 87 Station Street, Swinton. He then left the employ of the Wentworth Estate and opened up his own building contractors. He proved very successful and was the builder of many of the finer buildings erected during the transition of Swinton from a village to a town.

He built the Swinton Bridge School, the Roman Terrace School, the Swinton Co-operative buildings as well as many individual houses and cottages. He also built Temperance Street for the Otters and Highthorn Villas, the latter being built as a self development. He acquired various pieces of land, some of which he farmed. He also bought the land and erected the development known as "The Villas" at the rear of "The Sportsman" public house on Fitzwilliam Street.

It is believed he most likely had bought this land from Robert Otter. He moved into number 58 The Villas along with his family and a live-in servant, Jane Wood of Great Houghton. They had six children, Mabel Elizabeth, born in 1877, Edith Constance in 1884, Elsie Anne in 1886, Basil Cedric in 1892, Gwendoline in 1894 with Alice Maud being the last born. After effecting a sale of number 58, Joseph and Anne moved back onto Station Street, living at Number 154.

He had been building up his wealth and status quite successfully and his tenancy of the Hall was a final jump up the ladder of respectability. He moved into the Hall with a compliment of domestic staff. He continued his building business from the Old Hall stables on Church Street. He employed a gentleman named Smith as a junior partner to do a lot of the running around. Smith later went into partnership with the Trowbridges.

Although successful in business, Joseph was always very public-spirited. He was leader of SUDC from 1894 until 1896 and remained part of the Council for a further thirty one years. With the building of the schools, etc, there was a degree of nepotism that wouldn't have been allowed today due to conflicts of interest with his position on the Council.

Back in 1897, Joseph had organised a team of twenty individuals to organise the formal town celebrations for the Diamond Jubilee of Queen Victoria. The team included a mix of clergy, head teachers and councillors as well as local business people and tradesman. It was a task he would undertake again later in life.

He was an ardent churchman and was a church warden at St Margaret's for four years. He also sat on the Wath Joint Hospital Board and was chairman of the School Board as well as a governor at the Mexborough School. He was also a sponsor and steward of Swinton Cricket Club.

He, like the Otters, also sold the mineral rights to the coal companies on land he owned at Kilnhurst and Meadow View. He also acquired Hawthorn Farm at the side of Swinton Hall. It

A picture taken of the side elevation of the Hall, showing thick ivy growing up the walls.

was possibly purchased from the Otters as it was often known as "Home Farm" for the Hall. At the time of purchase, the tenants were the Lines family, who lived there for many years. It may have been with a view of moving into it in later years.

The lease he had on Swinton Hall stated that he had to keep the grounds in good appearance. Whilst I can't comment on previous tenants, it is known that Joseph Aquilla Bower kept the gardens magnificently and did so the whole time.

Joseph was one of the directors of the Mexborough and Swinton Gas Company and was chairman of it when it controversially sold out its interests to Swinton and Mexborough Councils. This situation caused the most horrobilis of Joseph's political career. The Gas Board Act of 1909 opened the doors for gas companies to overcome difficulties so they could expand their services to benefit the citizens with gas as a fuel. The original Mexborough and Swinton Gas Company was privately owned and was founded way back in 1856.

There were several investorsof the company, one of which was investor, Joseph Aquilla Bower. The legal advisor for the company was Swinton Town Clerk, Frederick Lee Harrop. In lieu of the act, it was decided that a new company would be formed called "The Swinton and Mexborough Gas Light Company". The assets of the existing company were to be

A picture of the veranda entrance into Swinton Hall, which still exists today. The only thing missing is the chairs and the ivy.

A further picture of Swinton Hall from Joseph Aquilla Bower's days, again giving one a glimpse of the splendid gardens.

transferred to the new company, the cost for which was built into a budget that would also give sufficient funds to expand the pipe network and build more storage tanks. The company then had to approach a special Parliamentary Committee to get the proposals ratified under the Act. Under the new proposals, the price for gas supplied, which had been unchanged for the previous twenty six years, was to be lifted from three shillings six pence per 1000 cubic feet to five shillings. People were not impressed.

Mexborough Council decided to attend the hearing at the Houses of Parliament, which was to consider the new proposals along with a petition signed by the town's citizens. They wanted amendments that:-

a) The price of the gas was to remain at 3s 6d.

b) The Council could control over how deep new pipes were to be placed underground and the route they would take.

c) A clause inserting that the share capital be reduced by £20,000 as it felt the spending of so much money would force increased prices of gas because of interest. It wanted a reinvestment of profits to fund expansion.

d) A new clause that the maximum dividend payment to shareholders be to a maximum of 5% so leaving good profits in the company to reinvest.

e) A clause that the company could be bought by Mexborough and Swinton councils or citizens for a discounted price of five percent lower than the market price of the company.

This put Joseph Aquilla in an untenable position as a director/chairman of the gas company and also being a serving Swinton Council member. He met with company secretary, Frederick Lee Harrop to discuss this action.

Harrop was also compromised as he was working as advisor to the

59

The gardens of Swinton Hall towards the rear end.

Swinton Council whilst also being company secretary for the gas company – a very unenviable position. There was no way the company wanted the capital restrictions or the compulsory purchase clause. They first approached the S.U.D.C before the meeting in London to see if it alone was prepared to buy the existing gas company. The Council Committee knew of Joseph's position as a director and that was transparent.

This offer was turned down by the Council. In the meantime, a letter to S.U.D.C from M.U.D.C was passed to Mr Harrop for due discussion at Swinton's next meeting. M.U.D.C wanted Swinton's backing for the petition. The letter was however, never read out or revealed.

Instead, discussions took place that Mexborough had a hidden agenda and a delegation from Swinton should go down to London in order that Mexborough would not ruin any later opportunities for the town. The Swinton delegation however, felt humiliated in London as they knew nothing of Mexborough's letter to S.U.D.C setting out their case. They in fact, thought Mexborough's proposals were honourable, and on the spot, made a decision to support Mexborough. If it had not been jointly supported, the Parliamentary Committee would not have allowed the amendments.

Back at Swinton, mayhem broke out at the next Council meeting. Why did the town's legal advisor not read out Mexborough's letter? Who was Joseph Aquilla Bower really serving, as his actions indicated for the gas company not the Council? If there hadn't been an act of support for Mexborough in London, the town's citizens would be faced with large price increases from a company Joseph Aquilla Bower partly controlled. Frederick Lee Harrop's explanation that he thought the letter had been read out by someone in his absence caused some frowns.

Joseph explained that there was a problem with leaks on the extensive existing pipework and major costs had to be undertaken to remedy it. Mexborough seemed to be oblivious to this.

The town was torn on the matter. Some felt that why should a private company be dictated to by Government as to its dividends and sale price? Others thought it was a massive injustice for the town. The fact that Joseph offered S.U.D.C the company outright so that Mexborough wasn't involved proved he was working in the town's interest. He told them, "I trust my conduct during the last twenty eight years is sufficient to prove I would not do anything wrong in a matter of this sort". Prominent citizens like Enoch Jagger came out in his support.

There were to be the new local elections shortly and Joseph offered to stand down. The South Yorkshire Times however, backed him and stated in its pages that, "Mr Bower is naturally reticent but his years of conscientious service should be considered to take him back into the chamber. He is a useful man and besides, building experts are rather handy on a building committee". He was duly returned. In 1909, the Councils of Mexborough and Swinton took a poll amongst the citizens to buy the gas company outright. The poll was in favour and the shareholders, including Joseph, received a payout of £74900. Strangely, Frederick Lee Harrop was known to comment he thought this price was too high.

October 1914 saw yet another tragedy at Swinton Hall in that Anne Elizabeth, Joseph's wife, died at the age of 57.

It was at this time that Robert Otter offered the freehold of both Swinton Hall and Swinton House to Joseph. Several years earlier, Joseph may well have relished the prospect but now, with the loss of his wife, he thought differently and declined the offer. Why Robert wanted to sell we are uncertain but with the advance of World I and his past military background, he perhaps feared the worst. Following Joseph's refusal, Robert made it known in the area that the properties were up for sale but there were no takers.

Joseph's daughter, Connie, married Frank Ward who was a head teacher and they moved to Gargrave, where he was in post. Following the death of her mother, an opportunity to return back to Swinton to help look after her father, Joseph, arose. Mr Peat, the headmaster at Swinton Fitzwilliam Junior School, was to leave his post as headmaster and Frank Ward was successful in getting the job. They lived in the part of the Hall nearest Fitzwilliam Street and known as Swinton Lodge to differentiate it from the rest of the living accommodation

Joyce Lines, as she was then (now Cavill), can remember visiting the Hall with her father and

Joseph Aquilla Bower sits for the cameraman.

recalls swinging in the outdoor settee chair, which was situate outside the main entrance. She remembers the large lawns and flowerbeds. Her father Ernest Lines was friendly with Mr Bower and used to keep a watchful eye out if the Hall was left empty.

Joseph had ambitions for his son, Basil and influenced him into pursuing a professional career. He took up articles to become a solicitor with Nicholson Solicitors in Wath upon Dearne.

When the First World War broke out, Basil didn't enlist straight away as he wanted to finish his articles and qualify as a solicitor. He completed these successfully and then enlisted.

It was around this time that Robert Otter made some of his land available for lease by the Council for use as a recreational ground for the town. This land was at Piccadilly and was part of the 1816 settlements made to the Otters. To help with the war efforts, he also made two acres available for allotments to boost home-grown produce. The lease finally agreed between all parties was for fifteen years with no rent rises.

A picture, believed to have been taken at Swinton Hall, showing Joseph Aquilla Bower with his daughters and grandchildren.

After the war, Basil Bower got the job of town clerk to the Swinton Urban Council with a starting salary of £250 per annum. It caused a few mutterings as he was Joseph's son, who still had very strong connections with the Council.

Basil worked every morning on Council business and saw private clients on legal matters in the afternoons from his house at Church Street, where the front room was made into an office. He continued as Swinton Town Clerk right up until 1948.

In 1922, Basil married Constance Bertha Peat. She was the daughter of Mr Cecil W Peat, former headmaster of Fitzwilliam Junior School. Politically, Mr Peat had also previously represented the town as an independent councillor.

Life at the Hall continued.

Joseph was known for his strong character and when Basil's son was born, he wanted him to be called Joseph. Basil and Constance submitted to this request but also gave him the second name of Cecil after his maternal grandfather.

Joseph Aquilla acquired a leasehold interest on a plot of land at Filey and Basil made a sectional wooden chalet in the orchard at Swinton

This is the chalet that was erected in the grounds of Swinton Hall and transported to the East Coast and duly erected as a holiday home for the Bowers.

Hall. The sectional building was then transported to the east coast and duly erected. Many enjoyable family holidays were had over the years.

Having a holiday home was then generally unheard of and in the infancy of this type of extravagance.

The Swinton Estate generated extra financial income for Robert Charles Otter in that further mining leases were granted in 1915 for more coal extraction by Kilnhurst Colliery. Unfortunately, nothing generated from the Swinton Estate was used at Swinton but it was simply used as a source of perennial income, which meant the Swinton properties were all running down. Mr Bower was responsible for internal

Joseph Aquilla Bower's son, Basil Bower, the solicitor. Here he his seen on Swinton Urban District Council business donning his bowler hat.

repairs but the external structure of Swinton Hall was still the responsibility of the Otters.

It is also noted that a Mr William Hague was also mentioned in a further letter from Mr Turner as being a long standing tenant of Swinton House and had probably taken over from the Fenners.

Marianne Eva Otter, the wife of Robert Charles Otter, died in on 4 January 1916. They had been married for 36 years. Within a year, Robert remarried to Mary Chetwynd who was the eldest daughter of the Honourable R W Chetwynd. He was considerably older than she was. This does seem to be very soon following his first wife's death. One assumes they were known to each other for many years previous. He was 67 years of age at the time of his second marriage.

Commemorative plaque to Marianne Eva, wife of Robert Otter.

Some of the land bought by the Town Council from the Otters had ancient tythes attached and these were not removed and the tythe payments on them continued to accrue. Robert had not collected these for some years and caused some controversy when he sent the Council, on 24 September 1919, a bill demanding all the back years' arrears.

This may well have been because the Council backed off from buying some land for housing at Piccadilly in favour of an alternative site. Perhaps he started to feel some of his father's past resentments for councils and boards.

One tenant who rented one of the Otters' properties on Temperance Street in 1921 was none other than William Arthur Morris, "The Pitman's Poet". He moved in with his wife, Julia and daughters, Barbara and Joan.

Barbara went on to have a daughter, who became known as Julie Andrews, the international star of stage and screen. I wonder if he kept the rent up? He left in 1928. (For the full story of Arthur Morris, please refer to the book, "The Pitman's Poet; The Life and Times of Arthur Morris" by Giles Brearley ISBN 1-904706-08-87.)

Periodic land sales continued right up to 1929 so that the Swinton Estate was, by then, much reduced with a small amount of land, the Hall standing in 2.06 acres and Swinton House and grounds.

Although following his inheritance, all rents and sales had been paid to Colonel Robert C Otter, on 2 September 1929, he prepared a Deed of Gift and passed on the remainder of the Swinton Estate to his son, Lieutenant Colonel Robin Otter. Robert was by then, aged 76 and this action was clearly a bit of forward tax planning to try and alleviate impending inheritance taxes on his Estate. "Nothing is certain in this life except death and taxes" as the well known saying goes.

The Deed of Gift said:-

"In consideration of his natural love and affection for the Donee, the Grantor thereby conveys unto the Donee in fee simple, free from any resulting trust in favour of the Grantor, the freehold property situated in the township of Swinton, in the County of York".

Swinton Hall tenant, Joseph Aquilla Bower died on 30 March 1935, aged 84, so bringing the continuous occupation of thirty two years in Swinton Hall to an end. At the time of his death, he was still a director of the Desborough Coke and Gas Light Company. He was also on the

The gravestone of Joseph Aquilla Bower found in St Margaret's Churchyard, Swinton.

committee, organising the jubilee celebrations of King George V for the town. Of the original twenty committeee members at Queen Victoria's Jubilee, it was noted only six were still alive, with Joseph being one of them.

His health had apparently been ailing for some time but his death came suddenly and unwelcome, as it often does.

His funeral on 5 April 1935 was attended by many local dignitaries including the town's councillors, the Swinton and Mexborough Gas Board, the Swinton Conservative Association, Mexborough Mon-tague Hospital, headmasters from Mexborough Secondary School and the National School as well as family and a large number of friends.

Upon his death, his estate was transferred into the Bower Trust with surviving son Basil and his sisters as beneficiaries. Basil took over the directorship of the Desborough Gas Works and would periodically visit the works.

It is believed that Basil was offered Swinton Hall for himself but did not want the responsibility it would generate. The contents of the Hall had to be removed so that it could be handed back to the Otters. The family took what they wanted and the rest was subjected to a grand sale, organised by Cox Dewar of Rotherham. Their advert for the sale ran as follows:-

RE J BOWER, ESQ., DECEASED

SWINTON HALL, near ROTHERHAM

VALUABLE SURPLUS HOUSEHOLD FURNITURE, OIL PAINTINGS, PLATED GOODS, ANTIQUE CHINA, ETC

To be SOLD BY AUCTION by Messrs COX, DEWAR & BEATON, on Thursday, 10th June 1937 as follows:-

ENTRANCE HALL – Carved Oak Hall Stands and Chairs, Antique Barometer in Oak Case, Brass Gong, etc.

BILLIARDS ROOM – Full Sized Billiard Table by Buroughs and Watts on Turned Mahogany Legs complete with Cues, Markers, etc. Oak Cased Sideboard with Display Cabinet over. Oak Dining Room Suite in red figured velvet comprising Two Arm Chairs, sofa and 10 Dining Chairs with Shield Shaped Backs. Wilton Carpet Square 22ft x 12ft 6ins. Miniature Oak Bookcase containing 40 vols. of Shakespeare.

DRAWING ROOM – Walnut China Cabinet with Buhl Ornamentations. Rosewood china Cabinet and Ebonised and Gilt China

The grave of Basil Bower, St Margaret's Churchyard, Swinton.

Cabinet with Wedgwood Plaques inset. 2 Walnut Frame Settee and 6 Occasional Chairs.

ANTIQUE CHINA – 5 White and Gilt Rockingham Plates with brown glaze on under side (Griffin and Baguley marks). 2 Brown and Gilt Rockingham Bowls (Baguley). Blue and White Wedgwood Jardinières. Jugs, Pin Trays, etc. Tea and Coffee Service with gold scroll and flower decoration. Part Tea Service, Dresden Coffee Service in blue and gilt. Very fine Staffordshire Dessert Service in puce and gilt with central panels and Cattle Studies. Classical Landscapes and Wilkie's Blind Fiddler.

ELECTRO PLATED GOODS AND BOOKS – Including excellent quality Table Spoons, Dessert Spoons and Forks, Dinner Forks, Tea Spoons, Cake Servers, Cases of Cutlery, Fish Knives and forks, Dessert Knives and forks, etc, and about 150 vols. of books.

OIL PAINTINGS – "Classical Landscape" attributed to Zucarelli. "Interior of Larder" attributed to Snyders. River Scenes, Still Life Studies. Landscapes, etc.

STAIRS AND LANDING – Tapestry Stair Carpets and Runners. Walnut Chiffonier. Mahogany Occasional Chairs. Oil Paintings, Engravings, etc.

CONTENTS OF BEDROOMS – Mahogany Bedroom Suite with 5ft 6in Wardrobe with hanging compartments. Half Tester Brass Bedstead. Tapestry Carpet Square 13ft x 11ft 6in. B & B Bedstead. Tapestry Carpet Square 10ft 6in x 9ft. Chippendale Commode. Chippendale Washstand. Pitch Pine and other Bedroom Suites. Single Combination Bedsteads, etc.

CONTENTS OF KITCHEN AND OUTSIDE EFFECTS – Including Dresser, Kitchen Tables, Stools, Sundry China and Copper, Wringing

Machine, Croquet Set, Octagonal Rustic Summer House with leaded light windows, Garden Vases, 2 Oak Hall chairs, etc, etc.

Sale to commence at 1pm with outside effects. Goods on View on Tuesday, 8th June, from 10am to 4pm. Admittance by Catalogue price 3d to be obtained from Messrs. Cox, Dewar & Beaton, Incorporated Auctioneers, The Crofts Mart, Rotherham. Tel R'ham 345; or at No.109 West Street, Sheffield. Tel. Sheffield 23354.

The John Jagger Era

The first thing that Lieutenant Colonel Robin Otter did following the vacating of the Hall was to take out a mortgage deed on the property, borrowing £1000 from Lucy Nicholson, the widow of Nicholson the solicitor of Wath upon Dearne. This was to be at four and a half percent annual interest rate. The connection between the Nicholson's and the Otter's had obviously been going on for many years.

He took out the loan to carry out essential repairs. The loan was outstanding until 4 February 1938 when he paid the loan back in full. He was, by this time, living at Ashdene, Kilburton Cross, Devon.

Following approaches by the mining companies, Robin Otter granted further mining leases for fifty three years on former Swinton Estate land for Swallow Wood and Silkstone Seams. Although they had been selling the lands off, they had quite cleverly retained the mineral rights underneath. "The meek shall inherit the Earth but not the mineral rights" (John Paul Getty).

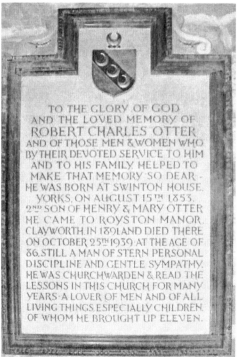

Memorial to Robert Charles Otter in St Peter's Church, Clayworth, who was born at Swinton House.

It was reported in the South Yorkshire Times in May of 1938 that while an old labourer's cottage was being demolished in the grounds of Swinton Hall, it was found that the bedroom ceiling consisted of a huge slab of stone, fourteen feet by seven feet and nine inches thick. It took eight men the best part of an hour to move it from position.

On 25 October 1939, Swinton born Colonel Robert Charles Otter died. He was still living at Royston Hall, Clayworth, at the time of his death. He was aged 86 and had been fit right up to two weeks previous. He even sat in as magistrate on 7 October 1939. His funeral was on a Saturday morning. There were to be no flowers or mourning clothes worn, which was a specific request from him previously. After the funeral at Clayworth, his body was taken to Sheffield Crematorium for due cremation. His ashes were put in the family grave back at Clayworth. The funeral mourners included Brigadier General Sir Joseph Laycock, Lady Whittaker, Lady Sibellargles, personal representative of Marquis of Titchfield, Colonel R Thompson and Superintendent of Police, W Boler, representative of the Chief Constable. There were also representatives from Swinton, the world of fox hunting and his other estates and villages of Clayworth. He did have Swinton mentioned in his epitaph to make it clear to all he was born in Swinton.

The tax papers of his Estate showed, despite his gift to his son Robin and family trusts, he still had landed interests in Clayworth, Swinton, Wath, Collow Abbey (Lincoln) and Yarthorpe (Lincoln).

His second wife had pre-deceased him in 1936 and so there was no tax free exemption on Inheritance Tax. But, unlike his father's time, the Inland Revenue were better organised and the tax hit on the Estate was vicious!

As the Second World War approached, it was to be the final end of the Otter's ownership of the Swinton Estate, which had lasted for one hundred and eighty three years. Suddenly, anything left on the Estate

Simple gravestone to the memory of Robert Charles Otter, situated at St Peter's Church, Clayworth.

was up for sale. All the land and properties were then put on the market. Local builder, Hoysius Bernard Tugby of Queen Street, bought much of the land around Bobbie's Row. This was split up into land plots and existing dwellings. It states on the conveyance that Robin Otter is still serving in His Majesty's Army as a Lieutenant Colonel. This time, the Nicholson Solicitors were acting for Tugby. Robin Otter's friend, Henry Farrar of Green Hammerton Hall, York, assisted by acting for Robin. The Hall went up for auction but there were no takers.

There was however, an interested party. Robin decided to sell Swinton Hall to Mr John Jagger for the sum of £600. Mr Jagger instructed Oxley and Coward Solicitors of Rotherham to act for him. Robin had already sold Swinton House to the Manvers Main Colliery Company who proudly showed their new acquisition for a sports club in their company accounts for 1938. The mineral rights were, again, not sold but retained by Robin.

Mr Jagger struggled to raise all the purchase money and firstly paid £200 and the balance of £400 on 20 July 1939. Robin Otter must have been desperate to affect a sale as there was a gamble in letting John Jagger occupy Swinton Hall without having fully paid up. For John Jagger, the purchase was to be a building venture. He planned to break up the Hall into even more rental units, whilst living in the best one himself.

The circumstances demonstrate the pressure Robin Otter must have been under. His father had recently died and he had all the problems at Clayworth that emanated from that. We were entering into a further World War and prospective property purchasers would have been thin on the ground. The

Swinton House Club shortly after the acquisition by Manvers Colliery Company Ltd.

72

John (Jack) Jagger.

price he accepted was less than the loan he had taken out the previous year. Assuming this was all spent on repairs (and the documentation indicates it was), he clearly wanted rid at any price!

Mr John (Jack) Jagger was born in 1888, son of John Incaman Jagger, whose family originated from Chesterfield. The Jagger family came to Swinton in order to obtain employment at the new Manvers Main Colliery complex arriving in 1884. On leaving school, John Jagger worked at Manvers Colliery as an underground pony driver. He served during the First World War with the RASC.

Harry Jagger, John Inkaman Jagger's second son, was one of the first Swinton men to be killed in the Great War of 1914-1919. On John's return to normal civilian life in 1919, he became local secretary of the "Active Services Fund" and helped to form the Swinton branch of the British Legion in 1927.

For some years, he was Legion branch secretary and subsequently, president. He became local secretary of the Transport and General Workers Union whilst working as a steel worker at Kilnhurst. He was a socialist at heart.

In 1929, he left the steel industry to join the staff of Swinton Urban Council. He retained his union branch secretary post. He served two terms as a member of the Council between 1920 and 1929 and then resigned to become responsible as the principle rent collector for the Council, a position he then held for twenty two years until his retirement in 1951. In 1952, he was re-elected to the Council and again in 1955 when he was the only independent Councillor amongst fourteen other members.

He was connected with numerous local charitable social and sporting organisations. For thirty years, he was the Red Cross Society secretary and at one time, president of the Mexborough District branch of NALGO.

He was actually connected with the Swinton Sporting Association and was closely identified with athletes mainly when the county cross country championships were held at Swinton and he was also associated with the Sheffield Harriers – a very active man interested in people and life in general. It makes you wonder if he ever had any free time at all.

At the time that John "Jack" Jagger acquired Swinton Hall, he was married to Jane who was born in 1883 and they resided at 48 Manor Road, Swinton, which consisted of relatively new Council houses. Jane was also very active in public service being a member of the Montagu Hospital Ladies Committee and was local representative for the National Institute for the Blind and organised all the annual flag days. She was also a member of the Mexborough and Swinton Board of Guardians and regularly took tobacco and sweets to the elderly gentlemen. She was chairperson of the Swinton Co-operative Guild for a number of years and was active in the Swinton First World War Welfare Fund. They had a daughter born to them, Eva Alma Jagger. She went on to marry a Mr Sanderson. Jane Jagger died in 1941.

It is believed that during Mr Jagger's early ownership of the Hall, it was broken up into eight dwellings and a variety of families occupied them over the years. The Goss family were long term occupants.

Plans were made in 1955 to raise some capital by selling off a piece of the Hall's grounds to a Mr W A Cooper, who planned to build a detached bungalow. After careful consideration, the Town Council decided to refuse the planning application.

Following the death of his first wife, Jack Jagger re-married to a lady called Ethel.

South Yorkshire Times: Saturday, February 4th, 196

DEATH OF MR. J. JAGGER

Active Association With Many Swinton Interests

THE death of Mr. John (Jack) Jagger, of The Hall, Fitzwilliam Street, Swinton, has taken from the Swinton scene one of the town's most respected and noted figures in civic, sporting, and social life. Mr. Jagger, aged 74, collapsed in Swinton on Saturday. He was taken to Mexborough Montagu Hospital but was found to be dead on arrival.

Representing the Council were Mr. Jagger served during the Coun. J. Randerson (Chairman) and First World War, with the R.A.S.C. Mrs. Randerson, Coun. Mrs. I. On his return in 1919 he ....

Newspaper announcement of the death of Mr Jagger.

Jack Jagger died on 28 January 1961. Swinton Hall was left to his wife to look after in trust for his daugther, Eva Alma Sanderson. For probate, it was valued at £3429. In his Will dated 29 April 1958, he left his daughter £100 and his friend, Jack Goss, who lived in the Hall grounds £25.

The Hall was to be kept in trust with the proviso that his wife, Ethel, could remain there as long as she desired. The balance of the Estate was to be invested with the interest to be paid to Ethel. Upon the re-marriage of Ethel or her death, the Hall and investments were to be passed on to his daughter. His widow continued to live in the Hall but later moved out to Chapel Hill, Swinton.

THE DEVELOPMENT ERA

One strange incident occurred in 1966 when a young Morgan Smith, a building worker of Mexborough, was working at the Hall. The legacy of the mining leases meant that the Hall suffered subsidence damage. Ceilings and walls cracked and doors ceased to fit in their door casings. Morgan was working for George Kirby Builders based at Doncaster Road, Mexborough, who were contracted to repair the damage on behalf of the National Coal Board.

Morgan and another labourer were working in a bedroom in the Hall. They had to erect a new underpinned ceiling and knock plaster off the walls in readiness for full re-plastering. When they started knocking the plaster off, they found a bricked up doorway underneath the plaster on the inner wall. The bricks were hand made and had clearly been there for many years. They used a sledge hammer to knock a hole through. As the hole got bigger, it revealed four or five steps going up to another door. They made the hole larger and went through. The door

Photograph of what was the main entrance into the Hall.

Unfortunately, these architectural monstrosities were erected in the grounds of Swinton Hall.

wasn't locked and they proceeded into the room. It was dark as it had no windows in it so they used a plug in lamp on the extension cable to light their way. Inside, they found a bed, a marble washstand and old style servant's smocks and hats. Their find was reported to Mr Kirby. It is not certain what happened to the artefacts or why they were there! From the age of the bricks and artefacts found, Morgan believed the room must have been bricked up in the early Victorian times. The clothes had survived as the sealing up had stopped air getting in and there was no damp. But why was this deed done? Was it considered that the room

A view of Swinton House taken from the roof of Swinton Hall.

76

was haunted? Had something gone off with one of the servant girls? We can theorise as much as we want but in reality, no-one knows for certain but what is for sure, it was a very strange thing to do! If you look at the upper side elevation of Swinton Hall you can see where a window has been very cleverly bricked-up in matching stone.

On 6 May 1976, under the Town and Country Planning Act 1971, the Hall and surrounding buildings on Fitzwilliam Street were given conservation area status.

Further coal was extracted from under the Hall in 1978, being extracted at a depth of 220 metres and 570 metres. Strangely, no application was made to the National Coal Board for subsidence damage.

There is no doubt that Jack Jagger would have been severely under capitalised for the responsibilities of being the freeholder of Swinton Hall.

The repair bills themselves over the years would be awesome and unfortunately, Jack did not have anything near the resources needed. By the mid 1970's, there were three tenants still living in the Hall but conditions were bad. Rotherham Borough Council became involved and following an inspection, they were re-housed. The Hall was boarded up and left empty. Director of Planning of the Council, Brian Moore, started negotiations with the Trustees of Jaggers' Will to try and negotiate a future. The conservation area status was a bit of a mockery because over the road, Highfield House was also boarded up and empty following the abolition of Swinton Urban District Council. It was agreed by all that the outbuildings of Swinton Hall were now beyond repair and needed demolishing.

Plan of proposed development by Ben Bailey Plc for Swinton Hall and the grounds.

It was finally decided to put Swinton Hall up for sale. The Trustees took the only option open to them. Before it was

Swinton Hall looking extremely dejected and boarded up following the death of Jack Jagger.

marketed further, talks took place with planning department at Rotherham who said they would agree a change of use to a hotel or country club as long as it saved the building. They also indicated they would welcome a Housing Association approach to turn it into many low rent properties. Unbelievably, they also indicated they would prefer this to a project by a private speculative developer. I can never understand why the Council seemed to adopt the attitude that anything cheap was better for the people of the borough than anything of quality, as is common in the southern part of our country. This is further exhibited with the building of two concrete low cost monstrosity maisonettes in the former grounds of the Hall when something of quality and style, befitting the area, should have been built there. Richard Bailey, Managing Director of Ben Bailey Construction Plc took a completely different view and entered into negotiations with all parties. On 10 May 1979, a contract was entered into with Ben Bailey Construction Limited to buy the property for the grand sum of £29000 including 2.06 acres and was so described as "the dwelling house, known as Swinton Hall with the outbuildings thereto belonging and all other buildings erected on the said land".

Ben Bailey, the Mexborough house builders, had seen the potential

Artist's impression of the development after completion.

for the site. They had previously carried out a full survey and after considering demolition of the whole site, formulated a plan for tasteful restoration of the Hall with an array of quality detached homes to be built in the grounds, something beneficial to the area.

It was decided that the Hall would be renovated and put back into its pristine condition, despite being in serious deterioration. The photographs illustrate the ongoing work and amount of restoration that had to be carried out by them.

The domestic wing to the Hall was demolished to create access onto the site. If you look at the Hall today, you can still see where the wing protruded from the side elevation. The chimneys were also reduced in height.

Another Swinton Hall mystery was a large stone safe that was found hidden away within the building during the renovations. This was covered in and no-one knew of its existence. One could only assume it was the then modern day equivalent of a safe for keeping valuables, jewellery, gold, etc, bearing in mind bank vaults were not commonly in existence when the house was originally built back in Regency times. There was a metal door on the front. It was four feet six inches high, eight feet long and five feet wide. There was nothing inside on discovery.

A view of St Margaret's Church from the roof of Swinton Hall.

Before completion of the site, Ethel Jagger died so sadly, she never saw the final outcome.

Ben Bailey put in planning permission to build the six detached houses, each one being differently designed. The land they had acquired with the Hall went all the way down to the stream at the bottom of Horsefair Park. In an act of generosity, Ben Bailey Construction Limited, on 23 February 1982, conveyed a Deed of Dedication for the land at the back of their proposed development to be set aside for the use of the public of Swinton, being size of 0.63 of an acre in size.

On this land today, Groundworks have recently put back part of the old fish rearing pond that was part of the original Hall grounds for food stocks.

The Hall was developed into eight executive apartments. They commenced marketing them on 13 August 1982 with prices ranging from £17,450 to £29,550 and were soon occupied and remain so today. Just to put a little family link into Swinton Hall, my brother, Michael, resides in one of the apartments and is a director and company secretary for the Swinton Hall Management Company.

Swinton House has remained in continuous use as a club since it was acquired in 1938. It was initially used for the management elite of the Manvers Colliery complex but other members could be admitted by personal recommendation of a member. The company built a tennis court in the grounds and it was extensively used and a tennis club was formed. At the first presentation evening for it, one hundred and fifty people packed the Empress Ballroom. The prize winners were like a who's who of Swinton society and included the Baker family (Baker and Bessemar Steel), the Hathersley's (doctors), councillors and solicitors as well as the colliery chiefs.

The club was heavily infiltrated with Masonic influence. Many people's careers were decided over a beer at the bar of Swinton House. The stewards of the club in 1945 were Thomas and Ida Keowa, who were very popular and remained in post for many years.

After nationalisation in 1947, the National Coal Board took over control. It continued in the same use but was also used for running management courses. I myself attended in 1974 when I was starting my Chartered Management Accounting career, which was under a scholarship awarded by the National Coal Board.

The club kept its standards high by insisting on men wearing a collar and tie at all times. This however, was abandoned in the late 1980's.

Today, the club continues but following British Coal's demise, its future is now in the hands of its members. I hope they now realise what a fantastic history the building has had and that they should strive to preserve it with tasteful restorations.

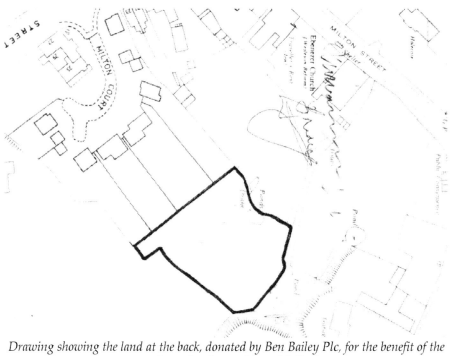

Drawing showing the land at the back, donated by Ben Bailey Plc, for the benefit of the town into what is now Horsefair Park.

Work on the surrounding houses is well underway in the grounds of Swinton Hall.

A shot of the safe, which was discovered during the renovations. The safe was constructed of large stone blocks wrapped in large iron bandings.

Looking up from inside of Swinton Hall following the roof's installation.

A view of the land donated by Ben Bailey Plc now enjoyed by Swinton's residents.

Groundworks helped restore the old fish stock pond for the Hall in 2005. There are many springs on the field and the water is constantly changing, so keeping fresh.

Development underway on the Swinton Hall site. The roof had to be removed and all the inside completely gutted.

The new roof of Swinton Hall being constructed.

POSTSCRIPT

So now you have it – The history of Swinton Hall, the history of Swinton House with some of the town's history all thrown in.

The writing of this book has left me with certain questions unanswered. Why did some of the Otter females in each generation not fare to well in the marriage stakes? Was it their strong personalities or stern looks? Or simply being an untitled wealthy family? The number of suitors was severely restricted from all ends. A lot of the other males also seemed to marry late to younger women.

I confess that in the past, I have drunk many a beer in Swinton House Club without any appreciation of its history but now, when I walk along Fitzwilliam Street towards The Traveller's Rest, I stop a hundred yards before Swinton Hall, which gives me a great view of Swinton Hall and Swinton House. Both buildings now appear as if they are non-identical twins and I think "Yes, the Otter empire".

Just think if John Otter had never married Ann Jackson in 1756, what would have been there on Fitzwilliam Street today? Fate plays a strange game.

It is strange that back in 1865, local residents were prepared to participate in violent demonstrations, risking jail, in order to get a vote when today, people with an automatic vote won by such strife, can't even be bothered to use it.

The completed houses and the grounds of Swinton Hall today.

Michael Brearley, one of the residents of Swinton Hall, here seen offering me advice for my photographic accomplishments from the roof of Swinton Hall.

And what today of Royston Manor? Following the high rate of death duty that prevailed, Robert Charles Otter's death saw an insurmountable tax demand put onto the Estate. The Hall was emptied and the whole Clayworth Estate put up for sale so to satisfy the infernal tax that was then the scurge of the gentry, although today it has become a burden for many in everyday life, not just the aristocracy minority. Following an earlier conversion to a free house and hotel with conference and restaurant facilities, Clayworth was put up for sale in December 1976 along with four and a half acres of land. Planning had been obtained to convert the outbuildings into more hotel rooms. Henry Spencer's marketed it for the sum of £50,000. It is today, back as a private residence with other dwellings in the grounds. Other than being acknowledged in the Church, the long association of the Otters and Clayworths is now just history – nothing lasts for ever.

A few years later, the Otter descendants apparently all met at the Church and held a special remembrance service for family members but no-one I asked seemed to know how to contact them.

Joseph Aquilla Bower would have been ostricised today for cornering corporation building contracts whilst being a serving councillor but there was a lot more trust and loyalty then. One thing that is sure is what he designed, he built well. He built with quality and he built in style. That is more than can be said for some of today's architectural designs implanted within the town's curtailage.

Swinton Hall couldn't have dropped into better hands than Ben Bailey Plc. They have sympathetically restored it to such a high standard and showed continued ongoing support for structural repairs. It will remain as a reminder of the town's history for many years to come – well done!

Appendix I – The Marriage of Isabella Otter to Leonard Swain Mortlock Marsh – May 1886

Wedding Present List

Benares Tea Tray	Mrs F B Prinsep
Silver Tea Pot	Mrs E Terry
Set of Apostles' Spoons	Mrs Foster
Set of Silver Coffee Spoons	Mrs Belce
Set of Silver Tea Spoons	Mrs G W Chambers
Case of Silver Sugar Spoons	Miss B T Cooke
Silver Mustard Pot, Silver Pepper Castor, Silver Salt Cellars & Silver Butter Dish and Knife	Mrs Warde-Aldam
Antique Silver Cup	
Two Silver Ornamental Spoons & Two Silver Gilt Forks and Spoons	Miss C Otter
Silver Breakfast Cruet	Mr and Mrs Algernon Bevan
Pair of Muffineers	Miss Pyke
Silver Mounted Claret Jug	Misses Fullerton
Case of Silver Knives and Forks	Mr and Mrs C Marsh
Set of Silver Fish Knives and Forks	Mr G N Powell
One Dozen Queen Anne Silver Tea Spoons, Queen Anne Silver Sugar Basin, Queen Anne Silver Cream Jug, & Antique Silver Milk Jug	Mrs Welby
Cheque	Reverend C Terry
Antique Diamond Ring	Miss A M Otter
Diamond and Sapphire Brooch	Mr E Wilkinson
Brooch of Diamond Swallows	
Old Oak Furniture (tables, cupboards, chairs, corner cupboard and stand)	Mrs Godfrey Armytage
Inlaid Table and Looking Glass	Miss A L Otter
Mirror in Old Oak Frame	Sir J Tilley, KCB
Grandfather Clock	Miss Tilley
House Linen	Reverend H and Mrs Marsh
Set of Persian Rugs	Mrs Bowen-Cooke
Embroidered Toilet Covers	Miss Evelyn Cooke
Set of Hem Stitched Linen Sheets, Pillow Cases & Tea Gown from Maderia	Mrs R Eyre
Set of Embroidered Towels	Mrs Marsh
Six Pillow Cases	Mrs Hambledon
Two Crotched Chair Backs	Mrs Hill
Pair of Slippers	Miss M Foster
Set of Glass Cloths	Mrs R Smith

Toilet Covers	Mrs Booth
Copper Tea Kettle	Mr and Mrs Hirst
Brass Tea Kettle	Rev H and Mrs Sheppard
Small Tea Kettle	Mr Noel Marsh
Brass Set for Writing Table	Misses Mahon
Brass Lamp	Miss Partington
Brass Dragon Candlesticks	
Brass Girandoles	Miss Beloe
Brass Bread Scoop and Tray	
Cheque	
Set of Brass Hot Water Cans	Mr and Mrs B C Otter
Brass Clock	
Silver Mounted Oak Tankard)	
Venetian Claret Glasses	Miss Shand
Venetian Salad Cruet	Miss Beloe
Caraje and Glasses	Miss Beloe
Set of Table Glasses	Miss Eyre
Set of Cut Glass Glasses	Mr Wilkinson
Glass Mural Mirrors and Vase	Miss Levett
China Dinner Service	
Oriental Dessert Service	
Rockingham Breakfast Set	
Rockingham Tea Service	Misses Annie and May Barlow
China Tea Service	
Dresden Coffee Set	
Two China Plates	
Pair of Dinner Candlesticks	Cannon and Mrs Leigh Bennett
Pair of China Dinner Vases	Miss Sheppard
China Toilet Service	
China Breakfast Cruet	Presented by the Tenants
Cut Glass Butter Dish	
Pair of Two Tier Glass Vases	The Gardner
Glass Boat on Mirror Mounted in Plush	The Lady's Maid
Pair of Ruby Tulip Vases	The Cook
Pair of Hand Painted Vases	The Parlour Maid
Diaries Bound in Kid	
Brass Ink Stand	Mrs Cooke
Waiting Folio	
Olive Wood Inkstand (in shape of wheel barrow)	
Pen and Pencil Rack	
Coachman and Mrs Bisby	

Newspaper Rack	Miss Caroline Nuttall
Brass Jardinere	Miss Cripps
Salisbury Tea Kettle	Mr and Mrs Dewe
Old English Glass Cream Jug	The Coachman (Bartley Grange)
Watch and Ring Stand	The Servants (Bartley Grange)
Garden Tea Table and Chairs	Miss A M Otter
China Jugs	Mrs Barlow
Pair Hand Painted China Candlesticks	Mrs Baguley
Glass Fruit Bowl, Sugar and Cream Bowl	Mrs Baguley
Pair of Buck Horn Handle Carvers	Miss Chambers
Case of Silver Dessert Spoons	
Two Little Glass Swans	"Jack" and "Jill"
Old Inlaid Tea Tray	Mr Groom
Olive Wood Tea Table	
Silver Claret Jug	
Mr R H and Mrs Otter	
Silver Inkstand	
Silver Candlesticks	Rev John Otter
Ruby Glass Bowls	"Rachel"
Cat's Eye Brooch	Mrs A W W Davies
Breakfast Cruet	Walter H Davies
Brass Stand	Miss Pettiwand
Brass Coal Scuttle	
Large China Bowl	

And many other charming presents, numbering in all, 100.

WEDDING PRESENT LIST

Afternoon Tea Table	Mr, Mrs and Miss Partington
Pair of Flower Glasses	Mrs Blomefield
Lamp Shade and Lily Pin Cushion	Miss Jubb
Card Case	Miss Lloyd
China Dumbwaiter	Mrs Otter
Copper and Brass Tea Kettle and Tea Pot	Mrs Francis Otter
Silver Button Book	Miss Ainsley & Miss Maud Ainsley
Brass Candelabras	Rev Reginald and Mrs Gatty
Silver and Ebony Antique Punch Ladle	Mrs Scrubb and Mrs Peel
Picture	Mrs Lloyd Russell
Picture	Rev Lloyd Russell
China Inkstand and Pen Stand	Fannie Bareham
Cut Glass Sugar Basin and Cream Jug	Mr and Mrs Baguley
Old Silver & Dutch Tea Spoons and Cream Jug	Mrs Cooke-Yarborough
Silver and Ebony Button Hook	Sir William and Lady Mahon
Painted Glass Photo Frame	Miss Mary Levett
Silk Cushion	Canon and Mrs Leigh-Bennett
Afternoon Tea Table	Rev and Mrs F Sheppard
Persian Rugs and Japanese Bead Curtains	Miss Otter
Leeds China Dessert Dishes	Rev and Mrs Henry Marsh
Blue China Bowls	Mrs Foster
Brass Gipsy Kettle	Misses Pettiwards
Japanese Bedroom Breakfast Set and Tray	Miss Ethel Marsh
Plush and Silk Tea Gown and Fur Boa	Miss Catherine Otter
Silver Button Hook	Mrs and the Misses Robertson
Silver Waistband Buckle	Mrs Arthur Durnford
Silver Dutch Sugar Spoons	Mrs Warde-Aldam
China Flower Basket	Miss Nita Remfrey
Afternoon Tea Dumbwaiter	Miss C Stevens
Roman China Tea Vases	Rev C A And Mrs Stevens
Silver Sugar Sifter and Tongs	
Silver Mounted Paper Knife	Lady Deston
Benares Brass Tea Tray	Miss Cooke
Embroidered Toilet Cover and Afternoon Tea Cloth	Miss Evelyn Cooke
Bedroom Breakfast ERvice	Mr and Mrs P Shelley
Pair of Japanese Vases	Miss Shand
Wedgwood Breakfast Service	Mr and Mrs H P Chambers

Toilet Covers	Mrs Booth
Cut Glass Dishes	Mary Booth
Japanese Work Basket & Pair of Footstools	Mrs Bowen Cooke
Photograph Screen	Mrs F B Prinsess
Munich Tea Tablecloth	Mrs Edward Lloyd
Silver Button Hook	Mr Kone, Mr M and Mr Ivor Gatty
Sugar Basin and Tongs	Rev R and Mrs Germon
Picture	Rev Mr and Mrs Dodsworth
Oak Chair	Mrs Eyre
Sugar Basin and Sifter	Mrs Pyke
Bird Organ	Miss Catherine Otter
Painted Glass Photo Frame	Rev P and Mrs Houghton
Bread Knife	Misses Leigh-Bennett
Silver Muffineer	Miss Eyre
Copper Tea Kettle	Mrs Hambledon
Brass Plate Warmer	Mr Hambledon
Opal Glass Vase	Mrs Grey
Silver Mounted Claret Jug	Mr Hawkesley
Silver Topped Cut Glass Scent Bottle	Mrs Durnford
Embroidered Silk Tablecloth	Miss Holland
Hand Painted Wedding Card	Nurse Mullenger
Diamond Ring	Mr R H Otter
Buckhorn and Silver Carvers	Dr and Mrs Clarke
Volume of Wordsworth's Poems with Photos	Mr and Mrs Beckett-Nicholson
Embroidered Linen Toilet Cover	Miss Balls
Opal Glass Basket	Mrs James Grey
Old Silver Spoons	Mr Walter Durnford
Ivory Paper Cutter	Mr and Mrs H Walker
Oak Bookshelf	Mrs W Baxter
Embroidered Linen Afternoon Teacloth	Miss Durnford
Indian Rugs	Mrs E Bowen-Cooke
Pair of Old Plated Candlesticks	Miss Catherine Otter
Silver Pepper Pot	Misses Chambers
Antique Inkstand	Mrs Chambers
Worked Silk Bookmark	Mrs Avery
Olive Wood Letter Rack	Mr and Mrs Gibbon
Pincushion and Toilet Mats	Mrs Collins
Macrame Wall Pockets	Mrs Johnson
Set of Green Wine Glasses	Mrs Creaser
China Butter Dish and Knife to Match	Mrs Hylton
Embroidered Linen Toilet Case	Miss Belk

Oak Bracket	Mr Belk
Volume of Great Painters	Rev H and Mrs Heap
Engraving by Frank Dicksee	Mr and Mrs Stevens
Complete Set of Table Glass	Mr and Mrs G Walker
Buckhorn and Silver Carvers	Mr and Mrs Rhodes
Set of Dessert Spoons	Rev and Mrs Ruthyen-Pym
Case of Fish Knives and Forks	Mr and Mrs R H Otter
Pair of Door Porters	Mrs Howland
Sponge and Sponge Basket	Mrs Jones
Carved Bracket	Mr Jones
Diamond Pin	Mr and Mrs Leonard Marsh
Oak Over-Mantel	Miss Otter
Painted Glass Frame	Miss Marsh
Pearl Horseshoe Brooch	Lady Weston
Pocket Handkerchief Sachet	Mr, Mrs and Miss White
Set of Lace Handkerchiefs	Mr and Mrs Thompson
Linen Afternoon Tablecloths	Mrs Godfrey-Armytage
Pearl Brooch	Mrs John Durnford
Crystal Salad Bowl and Servers	Rev H and Mrs Macnaghten
Brass Jar	Dr and Mrs Prescott-Roberts
Silver Sugar Castor	Admiral and Mrs Douglas
Cheese Scoop	Miss Mugget and Miss Thompson
Toast Rack	Mr Waring